Creation out

Don Cupitt

CREATION
OUT OF
NOTHING

SCM PRESS
London

TRINITY PRESS INTERNATIONAL
Philadelphia

First published 1990

SCM Press Ltd
26–30 Tottenham Road
London N1 4BZ

Trinity Press International
3725 Chestnut Street
Philadelphia, Pa. 19104

British Library Cataloguing in Publication Data

Cupitt, Don
Creation out of nothing.
1. Christian doctrine. Creation
I. Title
231.765

ISBN 0–334–02463–3

Library of Congress Cataloging-in-Publication Data

Cupitt, Don.
Creation out of nothing / Don Cupitt.
p.   cm.
Includes bibliographical references and index.
ISBN 0–334–02463–3
1. Creation. 2. Religion—Philosophy. 3. Nihilism
(Philosophy). 4. Word of God (Theology). 5. Languages—
Religious aspects—Christianity. I. Title.
BT695.C87   1990
213—dc20   90–38813

Typeset by Gloucester Typesetting Services, Stonehouse, Glos.

Printed in England by Clays Ltd, St Ives plc

For Susan

Contents

CONTENTS

Preface

This book is a philosophy, or an anti-philosophy, of religion. Its chief theme is the production of reality by language. Or, alternatively, the conquest of nihilism by speech-acts. Or the creation of all things out of nothing by God's almighty Word. I am trying to demonstrate affinities between some very old ideas and some very new ones, by way of making the new ones seem a little more palatable.

In some measure, people already accept that language creates reality. They know that writers create. They know that saying 'Done' may create a contract, and saying 'I thee wed' may create a marriage. They know that the world of the English differs from the world of the French by exactly the measure in which their two languages differ. They know that to increase your knowledge and your power in any field, you must increase your vocabulary. Articulacy is power. Your vocabulary shapes your world for you and enables you to get a grip on it. Conversely, the limits of your language are the limits of your world. All this, people know already. We add a further consideration: the end of the philosophers' dream, that the human mind could altogether outsoar the limits of language and history and lay hold of absolute speculative knowledge, is a great event. In religious thought it means giving up the attempt to transcend our myths and symbols, and returning into language.

A number of interesting consequences follow from all this. To give up the idea that there is a noumenal realm, or world of pure thought transcending language, is to give up the idea that our own thinking is anything more than the language in which it is conducted. 'Pure thought', so-called, is merely a movement of words that are not quite spoken out loud. And if, like religious thought, God's own thought and his Word of self-revelation are also just the language in which they are expressed, then we need a philosophy of scripture to explore the relation between the Word of God once spoken and the Word of God now written. We soon find out why there has never in the past been such a philosophy of scripture, for as soon as it is formulated it returns God into language. Like us, God is made only of words. So, as we are returned into language and God is returned into language, a new sort of theology and a new doctrine of creation begin to emerge. For we can no longer distinguish clearly between the sense in which God creates, the sense in which language does, and the sense in which we do. The religious life becomes a continuous flowing creative process, a little like art: humanly constructed and constructing, of course, yet retaining its own special place and authority in our lives.

So this book opens a further stage in an enterprise on which I have been engaged for some years: the task of describing an entirely post-dogmatic and non-supernatural religion of the future. A new mutation of Christianity is urgently awaited by everyone who believes that we need a religion, but that we don't need fundamentalism. We must try to produce it.

After the non-realism and the postmodernism of recent years where are we going next? My answer is something that I call 'expressionism', and this is a first instalment of it. Meanwhile, thanks to Linda Allen for typing, and to Hugh Rayment-Pickard for help with the proofs.

D.C.

I

CREATING THE WORLD
OUT OF NOTHING

1. Memphis

The phrase 'spitting image', still in use in modern English, preserves a group of very ancient ideas. Male semen was once thought of as charged with sacred causal and creative power, for by ejaculating his semen a man could apparently project out and create a small image of himself, his offspring. But human spittle resembles semen, and is associated with the mouth, the tongue, the teeth and the lips, by which speech is formed. And as a productive, forming and organizing principle, speech is even more powerful than semen. Through speech we express ourselves, thoughts formed deep in our hearts emerging through the tongue to control the self, guide social life and organize the world of experience. So spittle, because of its associations metaphorical and metonymic both with semen and with speech, has been widely credited with magical properties. A spitting image is a likeness so close that it could have been produced by one's own semen/spittle. And spittle is used around the world to form things, and in healing.[1] By extension, spewing and spitting may also express rejection and hostility.[2]

These ideas figure prominently in some of the very oldest creation stories known to us. Utterance 600 of the Pyramid Texts, dating from about 2400 BC in Old Kingdom Egypt, tells us that the creator-god Atum began his work by spitting out of his mouth Shu and Tefenet.[3] Both names have some etymological link with spittle, but in fact Shu was the atmosphere and his consort Tefenet was moisture or mist. So at this very undifferentiated stage of cosmic history we are to imagine no more than a cloud or mist drifting through the void. Only at the next stage of creation does Shu separate Nut, the feminine sky, from Geb, the masculine earth, so as to open a space for life to appear between them.

This creation-story was told in the great Temple at Hermopolis, where pilgrims could see the actual site of the creation of the world, a hillock rising out of a small pool surrounded by a rectangular wall. According to another account the god had created by sitting on this primal Mound and masturbating. From his semen had sprung the set of four pairs of divinities who with him made up the entire Ennead (Atum, Shu-Tefenet, Geb-Nut, Osiris-Isis, Seth-Nephthys).

A more primitive variant is also reported: Atum, it is said, created his four pairs of offspring by naming the parts of his own body (*Book of the Dead*, 17). This has some affinity with the very widespread myth that the world was created by the (maybe voluntarily-undergone) dismemberment of a cosmic giant, or a great sea-monster.[4] But more notable is the clear recognition of the structuring and creative power of language. By naming the parts of his own body Atum differentiates himself and brings new realities into being.

At Memphis, another major Egyptian sanctuary, the god Ptah was worshipped as creator. For a time in the third millennium BC Memphis was actually the capital city of Egypt, and its temple therefore needed a cosmology that would incorporate and go beyond the teaching of such rival holy places as Hermopolis and Heliopolis. The answer was given, it appears, in a sacred drama performed at festival seasons. Ptah was the supreme god who had created himself and heaven and earth. He was something like an eternal Mind. At the other sanctuaries the primal waters, personified as Nun and his consort Nunet, were already present before the creator took his seat on the primal Mound. Here in Memphis, though, Ptah is regarded as an absolute creator who creates out of nothing, for even Nun and Nunet are said to have come from him.

And Ptah creates by conceiving thoughts in his heart and speaking them with his tongue. The text emphasizes that this intellectual-linguistic account of the creation is intended to displace or supersede the older image of Atum creating by ejaculating his semen. 'Ptah's Ennead (of gods) are in front of him as teeth and lips which are nothing else but the seed and hands of Atum . . . the Ennead are the teeth and the lips in his mouth which has pronounced the names of all things . . .'[5] Semen had been only a metaphor for the true creator, which is speech.

The Memphite text explains these grand ideas by referring back to the human physiology from which the theology draws all its metaphors. 'The heart and the tongue have power over all the members . . . the seeing of the eyes, the hearing of the ears and the breathing of the nose make report to the heart. And it is the heart which produces all cogitation, and it is the tongue which repeats all that has been thought out by the heart . . . The activity of the arms, the walking of the feet, the movement of all the members, according to the order which the heart has thought out, have come forth by the tongue, and are put into effect in order to accomplish all things.'[6]

Ancient Egypt is usually regarded as pre-philosophical, but a number of notable philosophical ideas have already come into play here. We explain the universe by drawing metaphors from ourselves. We picture the supreme God as a sort of linguistic idealist who creates by using language, *because that is what we ourselves do.* Creation is an act of self-expression. We create by drawing distinctions. The Egyptian myths suggest that the four most primal distinctions are the following: begetter and offspring, male and female, the parts of one's own body, and the cosmic regions. Language differentiates, names, creates, sets in order and controls all things. Even our knowledge and control of our own bodies is linguistic. Thinking is a form of talking to oneself, and volition is telling oneself what to do, giving oneself orders.

Finally, the Old Egyptian myths point to a very special sense in which language, and in particular the use of language to perform actions, is primary. Language comes first, its firstness being not

3

quite chronological and not quite logical, but religious. Many modern writers have maintained, first that myth is the fundamental form of religious expression, and secondly that myths are most typically concerned with creation, validation and origins. Malinowski and the English school of anthropologists up to E. R. Leach, for example, were keen exponents of these doctrines.[7] They were also highly aware of the extent to which magic and ritual involve expressive and performative linguistic actions. Put all this together and we have a new way of defining religion: it is society's way of ordering the creative and productive powers of language. The whole scientific tradition, from Aristotle (*de Interpretatione*) onwards, has tended first to be realistic in philosophy and then to stress only the secondary and indicative use of language. First the world is seen as being already there and already divided up into neat sentence-shaped chunks, and then language gets invented as a means of representing or describing it. There'll be one fact-stating sentence for each sentence-shaped chunk of the world. Where people think like this, they tend to see religious ideas about the creation of the world as would-be explanations, like our modern cosmological theories. Religion, they suppose, is merely a secondary attempt to copy and account for the world, like science. To this day there are theologians who try to link the doctrine of creation to the Big Bang of standard-model cosmological theory. But, if I am right, they are making a Big Mistake. For one thing, religious thought is concerned with ordinary language and with the middle of life, and has no need to defer to highly specialized and marginal forms of technical expertise. It is wrong to suppose that the physical cosmologist as such is somehow closer than the rest of us to understanding what life is all about; on the contrary, the meaning of religion is equidistant from each human being. And secondly, in any case the older religious tradition was right all along in that it presented in mythic form perfectly sound insights into the creative and productive role of language in the world and in our life. Language is the medium in which we live and move and have our being. In it we act, we structure the world and order every aspect of our social life. Only language stands between us and the Void. It shapes everything. The Forms of antiquity and the divine Ideas of the Middle Ages were all along just – words. So the old creation narratives were saying something important, and something we need to recover, about the religious significance of language and about the linguistic nature of religion.

2. Semitic monotheism

In semitic monotheism, that is, in the so-called Abrahamic family of faiths, God was at first a social rather than a cosmic postulate. God was the fount of social authority. He had called his people into being, covenanting himself to them and giving them their Law, and he was himself the secret of their identity, their invisible king and the ground of their common life. But ancient peoples, who were not encumbered by the later concepts either of an independent Nature or of brute matter, readily treated the Cosmos as an extension of the social order. So the idea of creation was easily transferred from the Jewish nation to the whole Cosmos, a small step, you'll agree. And as far back as we can descry, the emphasis was upon language. For, as social creator, God had created Israel by a complex cluster of linguistic acts which had set her up in a highly specific social relationship to him, laying overwhelming stress on his power, sovereignty and grace and on her corresponding duties of obedience and loyalty.[8] So this original social creation had involved a set of performative linguistic actions such as might be recorded in a treaty or other binding document, and when the idea of creation was extended to the cosmic level the emphasis upon God's linguistic acts was carried over:

And God said, 'Let there be light'; and there was light. (Gen. 1.3)

By the word of the Lord the heavens were made, and all their host by the breath of his mouth . . .

For he spoke, and it came to be; he commanded and it stood forth. (Ps. 33.6–9)

CREATION OUT OF NOTHING

By thy appointment they stand this day; for all things are thy
servants. (Ps. 119.91)

For semitic monotheism there is no autonomous natural order.
The regularity of the seasons and the appearance of the rainbow
depend upon specific linguistic acts of ordaining, covenanting,
promising, etc. that were recorded as having been performed by
God (Gen. 8.21f.; 9.8–17). The ancient Israelites were more up-to-
date than many of us, in that where we usually look at Nature and
see autonomous mathematical regularities, they saw effects of language. The regularity of Nature is produced by the fidelity with
which the speaker cleaves to his language. His word is Nature's
bond.

One's own existence as a person could also be seen as a product
of language, that is, of divine speech acts through which various
social relationships and tasks had been set up:

Before I formed you in the womb I knew you; and before
you were born I consecrated you; I appointed you a prophet to
the nations. (Jer. 1.5)

It follows from all this that the Hebrew scriptures themselves
are not chiefly interested in the question of whether God had
originally created the world out of nothing or had addressed himself to some pre-existent matter. In the intertestamental writings,
at a period when Greek influence had arrived and Greek-type
questions could be posed, conflicting answers were given. In the
Wisdom of Solomon a platonic sort of God imposes form upon
matter, whereas *Maccabees* seems to picture God as an absolute
Creator:

. . . thy all-powerful hand, which created the world out of
formless matter . . . (Wisd. 11.17)

. . . look at the heaven and the earth and see everything that
is in them, and recognize that God did not make them out of
things that existed. (II Macc. 7.28)

To this day Jewish writers say that *creatio ex nihilo*, though the
preferred view, is not a compulsory doctrine. The main emphasis

6

falls upon seeing one's life in the light of *Torah*, that is, as determined by God's linguistic action whereby he creates, commands, appoints, bestows value and pledges his protection. To believe in God as creator is to trust and to go by all the things that he has said-and-done.

The message of the Qu'ran is similar. God legislates to his creation, assigning to all things their various tasks:

He hath created the Heavens and the Earth to set forth his truth . . . (XVI, 3)

It is He who hath appointed the sun for brightness, and the moon for a light, and hath ordained her stations that ye may learn the number of years and the reckoning of time. God hath not created all this but for the truth. (X, 5)

[God] then mounted his throne, and imposed laws on the sun and moon: each travelleth to its appointed goal. He ordereth all things. He maketh his signs clear . . . (XIII, 2)

The world is the product of creative linguistic actions, and is seen as a system of signs which bears witness to the unity of the One who speaks it.

Of the three traditions, the Christian has been on the whole the most deeply imbued with classical philosophy, and indeed Greek humanism. It is also the only one in which creation out of nothing, both of the Cosmos and of each individual human soul, eventually becomes standard orthodoxy.

At first (e.g., Justin, *Apol.* 1, 59; Clement, *Strom.* v, 14) a number of writers influenced by platonism taught that the world was created by God out of formless matter. Similarly, many influential early Western writers (often influenced, like Tertullian, by Stoicism) held to the Traducian doctrine that the soul was material, and naturally generated along with the body.

Nobody seems to know exactly how the *creatio ex nihilo* doctrine originated. However, even human speech acts may create out of nothing, as when a king just by an exertion of his sovereign power creates a new post, title, rank or corporation. So *creatio ex nihilo* was clearly a possible development of the biblical idea that the sovereign God had created all things just by the word of his mouth. Like a super-king, he had called them into existence. He had named them, and there they were. Furthermore, early Christianity was intensely preoccupied with drawing doctrinal lines, and creation-out-of-nothing had the merit of excluding both the dualistic idea that matter is eternal, intractable and probably therefore unredeemable, and the pantheistic idea that everything is divine, emanating from the divine Being itself. Creation ex nihilo was a useful formula for maintaining the extreme asymmetry of the relation between the world and God; both God's absolute existence and transcendent distinctness from the world, and at the same time the world's total dependence upon God.

Put it like that, though, think it through – and it is incomprehensible. Imagine that I repeatedly say 'Frog!', and each time I say it a frog appears from nowhere in front of me. *Creatio ex nihilo* is tantamount to a refusal to put any causal links, or any theory, between 'Frog!' and a frog's appearance. The idea is magical, that is, empty and unthinkable, because we are forbidden to have any way of deciding whether the frog's appearance each time really is creation, or just coincidence. Unlike the action of a human king who creates a peerage, God's creative command lacks a regular institutional context to make its effectiveness intelligible.

Christ enters here as the mediating principle. From early times Christian thought wanted to say that God's agent in creation is his Son, his mighty Word in human form. Already in the Gospels we see taking place in and through Christ a conscious transfer from God to human beings of the power to perform divine speech-acts. The first, and the most emphasized, is the forgiveness of sins (e.g. Matt. 9.8). Many other examples develop in later theology, such as the sacramental formulae pronounced by priests.

Thus if Christian thought depicts God as a sort of linguistic idealist, it also makes the idea of creating reality by uttering verbal formulae more intelligible by humanizing it, by democratizing it, and by institutionalizing it in the church. In this way it looks forward to recent speech-act theory.

3. Idealism

According to much traditional thought the world-order we perceive was put there by God and is unchanging; but according to a great deal of modern thought the order of the world is imposed upon it by us, and slowly but continuously changes as our knowledge develops and our world-view is modified. According to much traditional thought God has ordained the entire set-up under which we live and we are in no position to correct it, but according to much modern thought it is we ourselves who have historically evolved the entire set-up under which we live, and if we do not like it then it is up to us to change it. We made all the rules, we are the creators, and ours is the sole responsibility for changing our condition.

Karl Marx wrote in 1844 that when the whole set-up is such that people's lives are determined from outside, then it is very difficult to free them from the idea of creation. Everything seems to conspire to tell them that Another has ordained the way things are for them, and they cannot alter their lot. But, says Marx in his *Economic and Philosophical Manuscripts*, on 'Private Property and Communism', §5:

> . . . since for socialist man what is called world history is nothing but the creation of man by human labour and the development of nature for man, he has the observable and irrefutable proof of his self-creation and the process of his origin.[10]

The claim that 'We give the orders' was first stated and worked out with great force by Kant, the founder of the German Idealist tradition in philosophy. It is important to distinguish three of the different versions of the doctrine that we create the world. The first says that we make the world by the way in which we *know* it, the second says that we shape the world by our *labour* and other practical activities, and the third says that our world is formed by our *language*. The first of these theories gives the effective leadership of cultural change to philosophers, the second gives it to politicians and labour leaders, and the third gives it perhaps to artists and imaginative writers. (Or to those who control the media; or to language itself, rather than to us its mere users.)

Hegel is typical of those who believe that the ordered actual world, *Wirklichkeit*, is not given to us ready-formed but is shaped by our *consciousness*. Thus over the centuries changes of consciousness produce-and-reflect the gradual evolution or dialectical development of reality itself. Karl Marx retains much of the same scheme of thought and therefore clearly still belongs to the idealist tradition even while he diverts it along a *materialist* channel. Marx maintains that there has to be a substratum of material stuff out there to give rise to consciousness in the first place. Matter is prior, and material factors always determine consciousness, but by our socially organized work upon our material environment we order, humanize, appropriate and even rationalize it, making it intelligible to ourselves and so making it our world. As used to be said of God, our making of the world and our knowledge of it are one. And our humanization of the world is also our own self-expression: we express and fulfil ourselves in the work of making the world ours so that, in Marx's highly optimistic vision, through human labour the world becomes something like a work of art.[11]

More recently somewhat similar doctrines have come to be expressed in *linguistic* terms. Language is the hardest thing of all to see, but it is everywhere presupposed. Language creates the possibility of subjective consciousness: I can think only in language, that is, thought is a movement of signs, a rustling-about of imperfectly-formed sentences just above my palate. Language is similarly the medium in which all our social business is transacted, and all our knowledge is carried. In language all meanings and truths are established. Only within and by means of language do the world and humanity get constituted as formed and intelligible realities.

These three stories about our world-making, Hegel's, Marx's and the linguistic one, agree in rejecting naive realism and in emphasizing a constructive activity that expresses itself through us. (I have to put it that way because, like Hegel's Spirit, language is bigger than you and me, more powerful than us and prior to us. We are just its temporary mouthpieces.) So, rejecting realism, the modern tradition insists that there is no One ready-formed Objective World that we see just as it is. On the contrary, and willy-nilly, our perception is always already interpretative and constructive. I don't first receive bare facts and only then interpret them. I don't first receive raw data, and only then process them. On the contrary, my interpretative activity finds the data and prescribes their form.

So we make the world, or rather, our various worlds; but out of what? Interestingly the old theological argument about whether God makes the world out of pre-existent formless matter, or whether he creates it *ex nihilo* and not-out-of-anything-at-all, is repeated in modern philosophy. Kant, who was steeped in Classical philosophy, was deeply influenced by the form-matter distinction. Just as according to the Greeks a particular thing is constituted by the imposition of form upon matter, so according to Kant the mind makes knowledge by forming, that is, by imposing general concepts upon, the raw unstructured data of experience. So Kant internalizes (or, more exactly, makes transcendental) the creation of the world. His version of formless matter consists of formless experiences. He calls these 'empirical intuitions' and claims that they are truly given to us. He also thinks we cannot build our world any way we like. In fact he spends a great deal of effort in proving that to build objective knowledge we've got to build the world in accordance with a certain pattern. Thus Kant tries to have it both ways, claiming both that the mind makes the world and that he is nevertheless still a realist, because we make the world out of a pre-existent matter that is truly given to us, and make it in the way that it has got to be made. So although it is only phenomenal, the empirical world is nonetheless objective.[12]

However, Kant's successors did not find it hard to see that his intuited data were like 'formless chaos' or 'pure possibility', so residual and so vague as to be on the brink of vanishing altogether. The empirical intuition is no more than a peg, a minimal starting-point. The thing that is known is entirely conceptual, and the peg to which all these concepts are attached – what is it? A *peg*, as such, already has definite form and spatial position. Such things must be thought away. Ex hypothesi, the empirical intuition that remains must be ineffable, formless, unthinkable . . . and so, redundant. It does no work. Absolute idealism followed, and at its zenith made the mind in effect as absolutely creative as God had been. In reaction Marx tries to turn the argument back towards materialism, claiming that there must be that substratum of formless matter for human consciousness to arise from and for human labour to work upon. But then in thoroughgoing linguistic philosophy a kind of creation of the world ex nihilo by language returns once again. Some of Nietzsche's most influential slogans, such as 'there are no facts, only interpretations',[13] come very close to it. So does Lacan ('It is the world of words which creates the world of things'),[14] and also the early Derrida, with his remarkable transcendental philosophy of Writing (arche-writing, arche-trace).[15] The movement towards an idealism-of-the-sign is still apparent in late Lyotard (Le Differend, 1984) and in Baudrillard ('the empirical object . . . is a myth', nothing but a cluster of writhing relations and significations).[16]

However, an idealism-of-the-sign could threaten a return to Plato's kind of philosophy. We don't want philosophy to recreate an occult spiritual world of semantic entities behind the manifest world. We want to keep all things on one level, up front and available to all. (Note what that implies: we can make the philosophy we want, we can make the world we want.) So we swing back yet again, to 'semiotic materialism', which is a materialism of the sign, or rather of the signifier. The two-level signifier-signified distinction is refused (one can refuse a distinction, a vital move just now), and we insist that there is only the signifier, its movement and its horizontal relations with other signifiers. So a (qualified) materialism returns once more – and modern thought thus continues in a new form the ancient debate about whether the world is made out of nothing at all, or out of some pre-existent and formless matter.

This brief review indicates a complex relationship between ancient and modern thought about the creation of the world.

CREATING THE WORLD OUT OF NOTHING

There seems at first sight to be a sharp antithesis between the old doctrine that God made it and the new doctrine that we do, and between the old picture of a relatively unchanging and divinely-ordained cosmos and the new picture of an unanchored, ceaselessly-shifting world of signs. The conflict is particularly sharp between the old belief that everything eventually comes together into One Whole Truth in the divine mind, and the contrasting modern denial of 'totalization' which sees reality as Truth-lessly and End-lessly plural, ambiguous, unpindownable and open to reinter-pretation.

The new vision is certainly extraordinary, and by historical standards profoundly nihilistic. Yet on our own premises, if we have talked ourselves into nihilism then it is up to us to talk our-selves out of it again. And our most ancient known myths long ago portrayed the creation of the world precisely as a conquest of the Nihil by the performative and imperative uses of language. Enlightenment thought tended to see language as existing to express feelings, to describe facts or to state abstract relations. It paid much less attention to words as deeds by which reality is produced and ordered. But more recently the cultural develop-ments that have also led us towards scepticism and nihilism have also brought us closer to very ancient and pre-Philosophical ideas. There is an opportunity now to join old thinking with new in a fresh treatment of nihilism, language and the creation of meaning and values.

4. What crisis?

The first philosopher to picture all of reality as one immanent process of dialectical development was Hegel. Like many other and later historicist thinkers, Hegel maintained that there was a sort of necessity in the way the world unfolded. The march of Spirit was a logical movement towards a final perfection of uni-versal freedom, consciousness and reconciliation. This claim that there were still laws, guaranteeing progressive advance towards an ultimate Goal of the whole process, made Hegel's innovations more acceptable by making it appear that he was fulfilling and completing the tradition, rather than repudiating it in favour of a fresh start.

Hegel can also, however, be seen as a radical. He was saying that metaphysics is over.[17] That is, the kind of philosophy that predominated from Plato to Kant is finished. Our new awareness of the historicality of human life and the cultural programming of every human mind means that it is no longer possible to tie our present knowledge and moral values directly into the eternal order, as if history and culture could be disregarded. We see now that our knowledge-systems and moralities are period pieces, historically-produced and not just absolute. Beliefs and moralities are in future going to have to be explained 'horizontally', in terms of their historical development, socio-cultural context and function and so forth. Although the full implications of this were not made quite explicit until Nietzsche, Hegel already points to a world in which everything, everything is shifting, horizontal, interconnected, human, a game with constantly-moving goal-posts, a world without any enduring and objective meanings, values or truths.

Is this nihilism looming up and making us shiver, or is it merely normality, the way things are nowadays and nothing to be alarmed about? Richard Rorty, in his *Contingency, Irony and Solidarity*,[18] clearly thinks that words like nihilism are overheated, and prefers the cooler term 'irony'. He explains the word irony by saying that each of us has a 'final vocabulary' to which we resort when debating the great questions of life and when trying to articulate our most cherished beliefs, values and moral commitments. An ironist is a person who – perhaps through living in a multicultural society and through having a strong sense of historical change – has radical and incurable doubts about her own final vocabulary. She's ironical because she has a dual attitude to her own deepest convictions. It is as if for her these things are certainties about which she is chronically uncertain, absolutes which she knows are only relative, truths which she knows are only true-for-her-and-not-for-others. She says: 'There are many other vocabularies, and some of them seem to work as well as mine. I don't see any truly independent criteria by which to judge that mine is the best one, or the truth. Anyway, I have found that my own final vocabulary develops as my life goes by. My beliefs and I are fluid, changing things. I don't have either a fixed position or a fixed identity. I am an ironist in that I am both firmly committed to my own final vocabulary, for in it I define my very self, and yet at the same time I am also uncommitted, because my final vocabulary and I are always open to revision and change.'

Rorty clearly thinks that in an advanced liberal society which is plural and changing we should regard irony thus defined neither as a plight nor as a spiritual crisis, but simply as a perfectly manageable and usual condition. We should give up nostalgia for the old days when preachers and philosophers reckoned they could tell us the One Truth and give us authoritative guidance. In advanced liberal societies the job of the moralist and spiritual guide is taken over by film directors, novelists and such like. These artists communicate in a rather indirect way through fictions, dramas and art. They don't *lean* on us so much as their forerunners did. They tell stories, open up new angles on life, disseminate new metaphors and new descriptions, and by these means help us in the continuous work of re-appraising and modifying our own final vocabularies.

As for putting into effect the new life-possibilities that art may open up, that is the job, says Rorty, of Utopian politics. In advanced liberal societies the work once done by religious symbolism and the practice of religion is done instead by art and political campaigning.

Rorty wants us to accept all this, to accept universal contingency and continual change and rethinking, without nostalgia and without any recurrence of the old impulse to deify something or other. He is particularly insistent that we should not deify language – an interesting warning against what he clearly thinks is a serious temptation just now.[19]

I agree with Rorty that we (that is, many people, of whom he is one, I am another, and you perhaps are a third) now find ourselves having to live without old-style metaphysical or theological underpinning for our final vocabulary. Yes: for me too everything is contingent, a product of history and open to reassessment, including all my own ideas about God and metaphysics. There are no guarantees and no certainties. Nothing is entrenched and everything is negotiable. Like Rorty, I don't want even to try to go back to a time when there were 'absolutes'. I differ from Rorty only in that I find that to survive, in our postmodern universe made only of contingencies, relativities and interpretations, I need more resources than Rorty's rather uncomplicatedly optimistic account supplies. We are confronting a world in which everything that is most dear to us may disappear at any time. Like us, all our values and our standards are rootless, fleeting and insubstantial. My beliefs and values have a history behind them, I can fairly claim that they work and make sense for me now, and I can give them my wholehearted allegiance. But I can't make myself, or them, or *anything*, immortal. And this realization of universal transcience is like the Buddhist Void or Nothingness. It demands something like a Buddhist spirituality and like an artist's selfless absorption in work if we are to survive. Wholly to be given to the utterly-fleeting calls for a very special mixture of attachment-and-nonattachment, an intense but utterly non-possessive love such as it takes a religious discipline to produce.

We can, I believe, already imagine a reading of the Christian Gospels along such lines. Consider the Sermon on the Mount, for example, as teaching that eternal life is to be completely and selflessly absorbed in the present fleeting moment. Creative love and creative work are a kind of ecstasy in which we can forget ourselves and escape the fear of clock-time. Or consider how we might reinterpret Jesus' death for us. Dying, he passed into the Void for our sakes. He saw the Nihil as he died (Mark 15.34), and his having gone into it then helps me to go into it now. We are all going to have to put our heads into the black sock, you, me, everybody. He had to; but his despair may give us hope, if we can but bring ourselves to share it. Dying with Christ in the practice of religion, we go into the Nihil with him. We experience it while we are still alive. We die before death, and are thereby liberated for eternal, non-egoistic life now. If I have already died to Death in this way, I can accept my own insubstantiality and that of everything else, and live free from anxiety. That is religion. It is the triad, life-death-eternal life. It is a daily practice of death-and-rebirth as the basis of a productive life. It is an anguished mortal joy in life.

Thus we may agree with Rorty that in the modern world nothing remains that is fixed or sacrosanct. Religion therefore now must be based precisely on that realization. It is a certain quality of life that we can reach if we fully accept universal contingency and our own mortality. Rituals are needed to guide us through Voidism and No-Self to selfless love and the reaffirmation of life. This practice of truth is not just for an elite, but for everyone.

Richard Rorty does not want us to deify anything, he says, but like a number of other twentieth-century philosophers, critics and theorists, he tends I believe to overesteem the imaginative writer. For him as for so many postmoderns religion has turned into Writing; that is, imaginative writing has become a substitute for religion as a source of inspiration. Here again I disagree. It was a misfortune that after the Reformation new Presbyter could so often turn out to be just as domineering as old Priest had formerly been, and it will be equally a misfortune today if the Preacher is similarly replaced by the Writer. We'll be stuck with yet another clericalism, this time the clericalism of writers and entertainers. Long ago Moses said, 'Would that *all* the Lord's people were prophets!' – and quite right, too. We don't want a world in which writers and entertainers do the creating for us. In the advanced media society everyone is a star or a fan, all products have to be attractively and fashionably packaged, and life is dominated by designers, trend-setters and box-office values. Too much designer-art, selling stars to fans, makes for a profoundly alienating type of society, and to deliver us from it we need a religion, and not just writers. In any case the record of writers as moral guides is no better than that of earlier clerical castes. No, we would prefer to see a world in which everyone is morally free, creative and productive in her own life. We are talking about a religious discipline oriented not (as so often in the past) towards loyal and devout acceptance of authority, but towards the conquest of nihilism, the affirmation of life, its investment with significance and value, and the production of innovation.

So we don't need art to replace religion, but we do need a renewed and creative religion to replace the religion we have. It will require a rich symbolic vocabulary, developed from the one we have inherited, in which people can test themselves out in debate with one another. And it *will* require institutions, for a reason that is worth spelling out. I am suggesting connections between religious myths about the creation of the world from the primal void, philosophical ideas of nihilism and the problem of how to overcome it, and the practices by which we ordinary people in our daily lives together make sense, make good, and make our world. And I am emphasizing the performative, creative, productive uses of language. God is the Word and the Word is God. But I am *not* attributing to language a mystic potency quite independent of society. On the contrary, the efficacy of words-as-deeds depends upon social conventions and social institutions. There are always rites, due forms of words to be used. So it is wrong to oppose the institutional to the creative. On the contrary, creativity always presupposes a social and institutional background against which it is exercised, and which makes it intelligible.

II

NIHILISM

1. The normalization of nihilism

Our language is still full of residues of the old idea that there is One Truth of things out there, which will in the end be reached. Scientists often talk as if they are sure that when a correctly-formulated question is presented to Nature, she is constrained to return the right answer. She has all the right answers, and one has only to find the key that will extract them from her. Others believe that history will judge, or that death will be the moment of truth, or that great criminals will have to live with their consciences, or that there is a side of the angels for the just to be on, or that truth will out, or that some injustices cry out for vengeance, or that tyrannies must eventually crumble and fall. There are dozens of such idioms still precariously clinging to use, and all bearing witness to the same great conviction – roughly, that it will all make sense. As in a classical detective story, everything will eventually fall into place. The loose ends will be tied up. Justice will be done and the truth will be known.

We have lost that conviction. Whatever it was, whether the pace of historical change, or catastrophic events, or developments in the world of thought, or just the host of different philosophies, faiths and ideologies nowadays jostling for attention, we no longer expect to see a culminating moment arrive when one lot will finally turn out to have been right all along, and the rest will be shown to have backed the wrong horse. We are agreed, now, that we'll never be compelled to agree about who is right. Our disputes are interminable because there isn't an external umpire. That is, there isn't a fixed intelligible reality out there, quite independent of our various angles upon it, and available to serve as an impartial umpire between us. We cannot separate our various angles upon things from the way things really are, and make comparisons to see which of our various human angles corresponds best to the way things really are. We haven't got access to an arbitrating real Cosmos, because meaning and truth belong only within the world of human language, a world of endless interpretation, commentary and dispute that we never get right out of. Only signs have meanings, and only a conventionally-ordered chain of signs that asserts something can have a truth-value. We do not have and we could not have access to any extra-linguistic and extra-human meanings and truths. We have to give up the idea that there is or could be a super-language, a language of Heaven and a Final Account. Nothing says that it must all add up. Nobody has the last word, because there cannot be a last word. Language and interpretation are endless.

Some people attack the doctrine that language forms rather than merely describes reality, because they think it suggests that science is not about anything. And they also attack the doctrine that meanings can never be completely spelled out, because they think it suggests that we can never be really sure about anything; whereas, they say, there are lots of things about which we ought to feel very sure indeed. But I can reply to this that nothing guarantees that anyone else is keeping the score, or cares as we do, or will at some future date avenge all the innocent suffering there has ever been. And *therefore* the onus is all the more upon us to strive to realize our values now. The doctrine that we are continually forming reality by our linguistic actions makes it impossible for us to pass the buck to 'the future', or to 'history' or something. It obliges us to be intellectually and morally self-critical. There is no ground for accusing a thoroughgoing philosophy of signs of being irresponsible. On the contrary, a philosophy of sentences reminds us that we are all the time passing sentence, and determining how things shall be. It makes us *wholly* responsible.

We live in a world of signs, for everything that is claimed to be a pure given turns out on analysis to be already formed by signs. Take that old favourite, the sense-datum. I seem to see a red patch: surely here I am indubitably in contact with something real and extra-linguistic? No, I am not, for this presentation is already a cloud of words and therefore of theories. 'I', 'seem' 'to see' 'a red patch', a 'presentation': the experience has already been framed, formed, constituted and made a conscious experience by these and other words. Take them away, and what's left is un-effable. Uneffed, anyway. Experience minus language is a pre-conscious inhuman unthing, pure chaos. Perhaps before I was inducted into the world of signs something that was before me did live immediately up against the flux of raw uninterpreted un-formed sensation. I was not yet 'I', not yet in theorized time and space, and the subject-object distinction had not yet arisen. When there was as yet no subject, then perhaps sensations had a pure and piercing immediacy – but there is no way now of my even think-ing this to have been so, no way back and no loss to be regretted. For Culture has since then written language indelibly all over my sensibility in such a way that what is called an experience is now just the activation of a cluster of signs. So the world's all words. At least, our world is. *Human* words. Even the simplest experience is already word-soaked, for it has to be significant or sign-laden in order to become intelligible. Since we can't actually understand anything but language, sensation has to be processed or formed by language in order to become intelligible experience. Even just seeing the red patch already puts you firmly inside culture and language. So quite straightforwardly and indeed tautologously, there is and can be no *sense* in the dream of getting outside the realm within which alone there is sense, namely the world of signs or language, and laying hold of the thing in itself. The thing-in-itself is the Void, the Nihil, the absolutely Other, the ineffable.

If there were anything purely given to us it would have to be called the primal chaos, or absolute nothingness. Think of it as white noise, or as a formless flux of minute events; what would be left of the world of physics if all the theory were removed. To make this flux habitable we must make it into a world. We have to generate order, meanings, truth, values, narratives. This we do by cleaving the primal chaos, establishing customary or regular distinctions between different zones and kinds, to which socially-agreed meaning-values are annexed. So we make the flux into a habitable world of signs, a cosmos. So there is a world – only it is not *the* world, but only *our* world, a cultural product. Chaos plus regular habits equals cosmos, the world of signs. Reading this, you're in it. And you are never out of it.

This cosmos, our world, is the life-world and our only home. Ordinary human beings live lives that are firmly centred in it, and rightly regard any concern with its supposed outside as being, precisely, 'fringe'. Our world, as it is portrayed in the newspapers, the cinema and the novel, the world of human communication and human conflict, is all there is for us and all there could be. There are many conflicting versions and perspectives within this world of ours, but our world as a whole has no outside as language has no outside, and no foundation or basis, as language has none. Indeed, our world is able to be a rich and meaningful world of signs only because it is shifting, unanchored and fluid. Sanity is to live firmly centred in a world that has no Centre any longer, but has become solidly grounded in groundlessness. At the end of the second millennium the life-world has just recently become profoundly post-ontological, post-metaphysical and even post-historical. We have entered upon something new and extraordinary that we must learn to live with: the normalization of nihilism.

2. Dogmatism and scepticism

How did we ever get to the hyperbolical position just described? Today's collisions between nihilism and its shadow, fundamentalism, derive from the old conflict between the sceptics and the dogmatists. In the Middle Ages the dominant clerkly tradition, rooted in the thought of Plato, Aristotle and Augustine, was realistic in the sense that it saw the human intellect as naturally made to know Being, the objective real-ness of things themselves. In time however this doctrine decayed and various species of scepticism emerged, the most notable being philosophical nominalism (words are just words; they don't grasp real eternal essences), developing into empiricism and observational science. For the newly-emerging 'experimental philosophy' appealed to the experience and in particular to the *observations* of the human individual. It was a view of things that seemed to picture the human mind as situated behind the organs of sense. Events in our sense organs, transmitted along the afferent nerves into the brain, thus seemed to supply the mind with its only input. But this suggests that we have no insight or deep knowledge of the real. We merely register the flux of phenomena on screens before us. We don't any longer pierce the veil of sense and grasp objective Being. We see only flickers on surfaces. And if phenomena or seemings are all we ever have to go on then a physical object will have to be understood as just a cluster of phenomena, and another person with a mind will have to be understood as a hypothetical entity lurking behind a certain sort of cluster of phenomena.

From the first, then, the new observational science was close to scepticism. To firm it up, philosophers claimed that our sense-experiences, at least when we are not being deceived by illusions, are uninterpreted pure natural data of which we can have infallible knowledge. By combining sense data in accordance with *a priori* rules, or laws of association or whatever, we could build up a body of well-founded knowledge of the world of fact.

So it was hoped; but the early modern age was a period in which the threat of scepticism was very formidable. Around 1575 Michel de Montaigne was studying the teachings of the classical sceptics which are reported in particular by Sextus Empiricus. As a result of his reading, Montaigne set a number of simple but disturbing arguments before his contemporaries and successors. Their effect has been long-lasting.

In the first place, it is argued that reason cannot attain to a real knowledge of Being because it is entirely dependent on the senses. But the senses certainly can mislead us in a variety of different ways, and at any particular moment may perhaps be doing so without our realizing it. So we are not justified in trusting either our senses or the empirical knowledge that depends on their testimony.

Secondly, for various reasons we can never be quite certain of the truth of any proposition, *p*. For (*a*) *p* is not self-evident. There are so many opinions held about everything in this uncertain world that we will always be able to find someone who disputes *p*. Furthermore, (*b*) such is the nature of human debate that a clever advocate can always counter the arguments for any particular point of view by developing an equally rational-sounding case for the opposite point of view. Debating societies indeed work by just this method of 'equipollence', finely balancing the arguments pro and con. Learned philosophers know that the world is apparently so void or so plastic that every possible philosophical position has somewhere or other a plausible occupant. And finally, (*c*) *p* can never be completely proved from its premisses *q* and *r* because such a proof would require us either to accept *q* and *r* (or *their* premisses) dogmatically and without proof, or to find *p* somehow already hidden within *q* and *r*, as in the syllogism. The only other possibility is an infinite regress, from *q* and *r* back to *s*, *t*, *u* and *v*, and so on forever. So nothing can ever be known for certain by reasoning, because nothing can ever be completely and transparently proved all the way back.

A third sort of scepticism, mentioned by Hume, turns on the unreliability of memory. Suppose I follow some long chain of argument or carry out a lengthy calculation. I cannot hold the whole thing before my attention simultaneously. As I trace out the later steps of the process I have to rely upon my memory to assure me that I performed or followed the earlier steps accurately. And memory is fallible. Thus I can never be quite sure of any multi-stage mental operation – even one like adding up a column of figures.[1] So in summary, there are reasons for doubting sense-experience, empirical knowledge, philosophical proofs and memory.

These classical arguments for scepticism are a standing invitation to dogmatism and to 'presence'. That is to say, the way the arguments are set out strongly suggests that the only adequate reply to them will be to find some immediate and infallible intuitions of reason or sense, or some propositions whose truth we cannot but accept dogmatically or which are indubitable. 'Presence' means roughly, 'unmistakeable immediacy', a pure and complete givenness which keeps out the possibilities of error that always creep in with mediacy, inference and the passage of time.

As for dogmatism, the case for it is an epistemological version of the political case for monarchy. People say it's obvious that there must be an ultimate authority, a final court of appeal, a starting point for thought. There always have to be some most-basic beliefs which, groundless themselves, ground everything else. The most vivid contemporary example is the role of the Holy Qu'ran in Islam. Once it is accepted dogmatically as the unchanging (and indeed, eternal) revealed Word of God, and provided that its interpretation can be kept under tight control, then a whole culture and system of thought falls into place and becomes clear and coherent.

Note that it needs to be possible to believe that the Holy Qu'ran really is God's utterance, the complete text in classical Arabic having been immanent in God's mind for all eternity and now faithfully transcribed at a particular moment in human historical time by the prophet Muhammad. A Muslim must believe that there can be a language of eternity, intelligible to us. And in general, the classical replies to scepticism depend on the claim that we can get hold of something extra-cultural and unchanging.[2] It may be a divine Word of revelation, it may be a rational intuition of necessary truth, it may be an intuition of moral fittingness, it may be an intuition of the self's existence as present to itself in self-consciousness, it may be a religious vision, or it may be almost any other intuitively-grounded conviction. It may even be just a pure sense experience considered as a natural fact in our sensibility and prior to any fallible human inference from it. Whatever it was, we used to think in our innocence that we were here in touch with something that was just *so*, something that lay beyond the relativities of human opinion and historical-cultural change.

Now, alas, we think otherwise. Now we know that all our supposedly culture-transcending absolutes are in fact just contingent products of history. They were formed in particular places and at particular times, and they will doubtless continue to be felt and to be effective so long as there are people who want them. People can be relied upon to make and to cling to the truths they need. But we have no access to a realm beyond space and time, and we don't know any language that is not a human-type language, historically produced and shifting about over time in the human way. Religious experiences are culturally-produced, so that from a detailed phenomenological description of *any* religious experience you can readily tell its cultural and religious provenance. But not only are religious experiences clearly the products of particular places and times – clearly, that is, culturally-produced – but so are moral judgments, sense-data, scientific theories and rational intuitions. Common sense is not timeless but datable. One only has to cultivate the habit of looking at all human institutions, convictions, productions and experiences in the way an antique dealer looks at furniture or porcelain, and the point is obvious.

So the absolutes, the certainties, all collapsed. Montaigne's own response to scepticism was to say that we should accept appearances undogmatically, live quietly and peaceably conforming to the local customs, and refrain from criticizing religion, for we lack the competence to criticize it. Personally Montaigne seems to have accepted the gift of Catholic faith (though there is certainly room for debate about his precise position). Quietism of this type can be traced back to classical antiquity, and it still has followers today.

All this prompts us to tell another story about how we skidded into nihilism. This time we will lay the emphasis squarely upon the cultural realm, and trace what has happened to the programming that makes us construe the world the way we do.

We start from the classical Greek distinction between matter and form, between raw unstructured experience and general interpretative concepts or theories applied to it – between, in modern terms, data and programme. And we pose a straightforward question: Where is the programme? What makes us read the world the way we do?

If there is one safe generalization about the history of human thought, it is that at first everything is regarded as being out there and built into the unchanging order of things. Then, step by step, what was regarded as natural comes instead to be seen as human and cultural. This shift is often, and perhaps a little misleadingly, called demythologizing, and is most typical of periods of Enlightenment.

At first, then, the intelligible order that forms the world and makes us construe it the way we do was seen as being out there. Everywhere, realism comes first. Pythagoras believed in numbers-out-there, and Plato believed in a noumenal world of Forms out there, each Form being the objectified and timeless Meaning of a general word in contemporary Attic Greek. Aristotle took a strong realistic view, not so much of the intelligible, as rather of the physical world. He, as it were, wove Plato's two worlds together to make a real Cosmos that was in every part fully formed. Aristotle's physical world is rationally-ordered and full of natural kinds, so that there is one objectively-correct way of classifying it. Finally, philosophical monotheism combines Plato with Aristotle. Plato's World of Intelligible Forms becomes the Ideas in the divine Mind. As for the visible world, it is an Aristotelian Cosmos, but not eternal as Aristotle believed the world to be. It has been created ex nihilo by God, after his plan and embodying the Ideas. That makes God a Platonist who has made an Aristotelian world, and it gives rational creatures a basis for arguing from the Creation back to the Creator. The programme is God's plan: I see the world as ordered because I recognize God's design embodied in it.

It is of the greatest importance to note that philosophical theism is, however, less realistic about the physical world than was

Aristotle. Pagan realism about matter taught the eternity of matter, but theists regard that doctrine as heretical because for them God at least is an idealist, the world being the projection of his mind and an expression of himself. It continues to exist only for so long as God wills it to do so. So it was not only platonism, but also orthodox philosophical theism, which contributed to Western idealism. As Aquinas puts it: 'God's knowledge is indeed the cause of things' (*Summa Theologiae* 1.14.8).

More of that in due course. We are still asking, where is the programme? What makes us construe the world in the way we do? In the early seventeenth century the new science aimed at a system of knowledge of the world constructed entirely by the individual human subject. The standard case of such knowledge was mathematical physics. To rebuild the world from the point of view of the human individual, using only the data and intellectual resources available to the individual – such was the aim. Human sense-experience would provide the only data, and Reason the only programming. In more detail, the programming consisted of a body of self-evident truths of reason, logical, mathematical and metaphysical, worked up and deductively elaborated. There was to be no arbitrariness, and nothing merely cultural, in this system. The truths of reason subsisted eternally in the divine Mind, and were accessible to us because we were created in the divine image. We can get things right insofar as our programming is a participation in God's own programming.

Thus the objectivity of knowledge in early modern thought still fell back upon the idea that a bit of us has access to a realm beyond space and time. The human mind participated in the divine Mind in a way that set up an analogy between physics, the science, as a product of the human mind, and *physis* (Nature) as the expression of the divine Mind. The programming of eternal truths in our minds was ultimately traceable back to the Mind of God, and the natural philosopher's conviction that he had a firm grip on Nature was sustained by the belief that he was thinking God's thoughts after him. The correspondence theory of truth thus depended on the doctrine of creation. Physics followed *physis*, the human knowledge-system copied the divine order, and the human mind was an image of the divine.[3]

Although he felt the full force of the sceptical challenge to it, Kant saved what he could of this old tradition. The proofs of the existence of God and the self-evidence of various metaphysical principles had been sharply questioned by Hume, so Kant freed the programming from its traditional theological setting and transformed it instead into an order of *a priori* concepts. It had a new status: it was 'transcendental'. By regressive analysis Kant proved, or purported to prove, that it had to be presupposed as a condition of the possibility of knowledge.

This was very ingenious. The programming that impels us to construe the world in the way we do was no longer grounded by Kant in the Mind of God, because that sort of metaphysical anchorage had become too insecure. Nor was it grounded in changeable psychological facts about the way we human beings happen to think, because that would allow scepticism back again. In fact, it wasn't really 'grounded' at all: rather, it was implicit. The programming was necessary and universal, so that there was no alternative to it and it therefore still guaranteed the objectivity of knowledge, but it was proved by a new autonomous and 'transcendental' kind of proof that did not rest upon a philosophy of God. Kant was moving a long way from Plato, trying to show that knowledge (and morality) could be proved objective without invoking any super-sensible realities.

The trouble was that the proof proved too much. It appeared to prove *a priori* that Aristotelian logic, Euclid's geometry, and eighteenth-century Newtonianism's vision of the world were all of them compulsory for all human beings everywhere, past and future. But most human beings, at most times and places, have been animists, not mechanists, and have got along fine. Still more important, *ideas have histories*. Nobody terminates the history of ideas, not Aristotle, not Descartes, and not even Kant himself. Indeed, soon after Kant, historicism established the point that the programming that impels human beings to view the world the way they do is not fully universal. It changes historically. It evolves. It is culture. The system of thought, the set of deep assumptions typical of a particular cultural epoch, may well appear to be *a priori* to the people of that epoch. To them it is all self-evident commonsense. But it may not look so obvious to other peoples at other times. On the contrary, the 'collective representations', the 'absolute presuppositions' of other ages and cultures are often so very odd that we are obliged to invent these jargon phrases in order to refer to them. The phrases admonish us that there are many and surprisingly varied ways of making sense of life.

All this has been explored and explained in detail by a host of philosophically minded historians and social scientists, such as Troeltsch and Dilthey, Collingwood and Foucault, Durkheim and Lévy-Bruhl, Mannheim and Kuhn. The philosophical conclusions were drawn most vividly by Nietzsche. Thought and being come apart. All guarantees fail. The 'real world' vanishes, as the programming at last becomes purely contingent. For now we realize that nothing says that the world has got to be the way society has programmed us to think it is. We may claim that our values and our theories work, but that claim is alarmingly weak, for every robust cultural system feels itself equally entitled to make it on its own behalf. It sees its good health as proof of the soundness of its own theoretical régime. Any and every powerful system of thought of course sets up its own verification-procedures, and creates experiences that appear to its own adherents to confirm its truth. Strong cultures don't doubt the reality of the worlds they create. To that extent, as Durkheim indicates, all vigorous cultures, religions and bodies of knowledge work and make themselves true. Montaigne's quietism returns: it begins again to look as if there cannot be anything better for us than to go along with the prevailing wisdom. Ironical allegiance to our own culture is all there can be for us.

We are ready now for the structuralist recognition that the programming is linguistic, and though it's only contingent there is no opting out of it. Culture is a system of signs inscribed upon us as we learn our mother tongue. Current linguistic usages carry our values and prescribe the way we must see the world. Society creates your world through you.

This vision is alarmingly bureaucratic, and post-structuralist thought attempted to break out of it so as to open a space for freedom. The endlessly fertile metaphoricity of language, the mobility and the unpindownableness of words, mean that we are caught up in language, not as in an iron cage, but as in a ferment and a flux. The movement of language is never wholly predictable or controllable.

In this most recent vision of things, the distinctions between fact and interpretation, truth and fiction, largely disappear. We are still language-programmed, but not in any rigid or deterministic way. Language and the world have become too shifting and fluid for that. We have come to the age of the cinema, and of the magic-realist and the postmodernist novel. 'Reality' has become a phantasmagoria, a magical illusion that continually shifts, changes and renews itself. We dream the dream and it dreams us, so we can dance with it.

3. Images of the human condition

What are we, we human beings, and what is there for us? Consider six typical replies, old and new, all of which have been given by people and groups of note.

(a) *Spirits trapped in the wrong world.* Ancient world-pessimism, gnostic and ascetic, Indian and Eastern Mediterranean, has maintained that we are aliens, trapped in these earthly bodies of ours. The core-self in us is a spirit whose proper home lies in another world altogether. If it seems to us that this world is so full of evils and illusions that we can find in it no lasting happiness and no true knowledge, then the reason for our discontent is that we have a dim but veridical awareness of being exiles, in the wrong place and away from our true home. We experience our condition as one of moral bondage. This world is so shifting, boggy and unstable that action cannot produce results that stay in place. So the only moral message that can be offered by an outlook of this type is: 'Do no harm!' The most constructive activity for us in the meanwhile is to buffet our bodies and purify our souls. Ascetical techniques which enact and 'hyperbolize' the spirit-flesh distinction do three useful jobs: they raise consciousness, on the principle that a divided consciousness is more intense than an integrated one, they give us an enhanced feeling of spiritual power as we victimize our own bodies, and they prepare us for our eventual release from this world.

It should not be supposed that world-pessimism is extraordinary. Something rather close to it remains Christian orthodoxy, and we can safely predict that before long it will return. Perhaps the three centuries or so of (qualified) world-optimism that we have just enjoyed will then be portrayed as having been merely a blip, a temporary aberration.

(*b*) *Creatures in a cosmos.* The first Christian millennium was in the main pessimistic about this present world, but in the second millennium there have also been some more optimistic traditions, which may be called Christian Aristotelianism and Protestant Commonsense Realism.[4] Such outlooks are more cosmological and ready to affirm that we human beings are truly at home in these bodies of ours and in this world. There is a real, hierarchically-structured, mind-independent, providentially-governed world order out there. The world is knowable and our life makes sense. The Cosmos is like a well-planned and well-run state, or like a furnished house for us. We can learn its rules and fit into it. Indeed, discovering your own niche in the whole scheme of things, and entering upon its rights and duties, amounts to much the same thing at every level – the family, the state and the cosmos. Hence the huge appeal of cosmologies of this type – familial, cosy, patriarchal, coherent and interlocking. How could such a vision ever be finally lost? But it has slowly decayed, as social theory and physical theory have reluctantly drifted away from each other since the seventeenth century. The upshot is that neither the old patriarchal nor the newer Green and feminist attempts to revive a world-affirming religious cosmology are now likely to be altogether successful. The various sciences, physical, political and so on, cannot be pulled together successfully, and still less are they amenable to being held within an overall religious perspective. But we include this particular story here because people's wish that something of the sort could be made to work remains so very strong.

(c) *Spectators of a machine*. René Descartes, an Augustinian Catholic, converted the old Western Christian type of self and vision of the world into the new scientific observer of the mechanical universe by a series of clever transformations. Spirit-flesh dualism became mind-body dualism. The monk's self-distancing from the world became the scientist's detached observation of nature. The monk's self-examination and quest for inner purity became the scientist's systematic doubting and testing of his own hypotheses. Since the self had long been regarded as a sort of finite counterpart of God and as capable (in heaven at least) of absolute knowledge, it was fairly easy to take the monk's aim of achieving absolute knowledge of God and convert it into the new goal of achieving a complete and godlike knowledge of the world. Most craftily of all, Descartes retained the monk's low valuation of the physical world. It was a mere machine governed by a very few simple mathematical laws, so that if one granted the monk-scientist's spiritual self-distancing from it and his godlike god-given rationality, the way was clear for proclaiming, without presumption or impiety, the possibility of a complete knowledge and mastery of nature.

So then, I am a finite mind, a purely thinking thing hooked to a body. The body-world is a rigorously mechanistic system of matter-in-motion. I am a thinker, a mathematician and an observer. By *a priori* reasoning I can project out the existence of the world and the physical laws by which it is governed. If I then fill myself in on the current state of play – that is, the current positions, shapes and velocities of things – I can achieve a sweeping, godlike knowledge. Not only can I re-present within my mind the present order of things, but also I can accurately predict all the future and reconstruct all the past. The Cartesian scientist can know the physical world just about as thoroughly as God himself does.

(d) *Agents in the Void*. In the last Section of Book I of *A Treatise of Human Nature*, written in the 1730s, David Hume confronts something like thoroughgoing scepticism or nihilism. All he knows, all that is given to him, is the flux of present experiences. He cannot find any justification for building upon and going beyond the immediately given by applying to it the concepts of causality, substance, etc., and so organizing it into a real surrounding external world. Of course everyone does do this, for we must do so to survive. But where is the proof that we are *right* to do it? Hume cannot find a satisfactory argument.

He was ahead of his time. After Darwin the agent-in-the-void vision of the human condition becomes a new orthodoxy. It is stated very eloquently by Russell in 'A Free Man's Worship', by William James in *Pragmatism* and *The Meaning of Truth*, by Sartre and Camus of course, and most forcefully of all by Nietzsche in his earlier writings. But although active, 'creationist' nihilism is commonly associated with thoroughgoing atheism, it is important not to forget that many passages seemingly expressive of the blackest nihilism are to be found in, for example, Kierkegaard. That is – and should it really be necessary to say this? – whatever 'God' be taken to mean, God does not always preserve the believer from having to enter darkness, despair, the Void and extinction. Rather the contrary, for it often seems that God, whatever God is, works precisely to tip you into such states. So, around 1900 or so, we find in Albert Schweitzer, Franz Kafka and others the beginnings of death-of-God interpretations of Jesus and what he underwent on the cross.

Darwinism, however, is of great importance. Darwin's enemies often grasp better than his friends how hard to deny and how ferociously bleak is his vision of the world. All sense of an external moral world-order, all purposiveness, all notions of progress, all belief that history or the future or something – anything – is on the side of truth and goodness breaks down. Darwinism is nihilistic in grasping that we are utterly and completely alone, with nothing whatever between us and the Void except for our own sense-experience and our constructive activity, our own needs to be met, the years we have left before each of us must drop through the floor, and such courage and will as we can muster in the meanwhile to affirm our values and say 'Yes' to life.

Nietzsche is unwearying in his insistence upon the need for strength and courage in the face of such a prospect. As he puts it, there isn't any firm, ready-made world out there independent of us. Apart from our activity there is only a 'fuzziness and chaos of sense impressions', something 'formless and unformulable'. Devastatingly, he asks: 'How could we know that things exist? Thingness was first created by us' (for these quotations, see *The Will to Power*, §569). So truth is the product of our own logicizing, adapting and construing, a continuous activity which must take ever-new forms. On Nietzsche's account, knowing, creatively forming, interpreting and producing truth are all different names for the same activity. The world is an interpretation – *our* interpretation – and it is plural and continually changing.

Nietzsche toys (*Will to Power*, §579, 4) with an even more nihilistic hypothesis. Only the creative subject exists. What appears to me as given is the effect of other subjects' constructive activity, their putting pressure on me. 'The other entities act upon us; our apparent adapted world is an adaptation and an overpowering of their actions; a kind of defensive measure.'[5] Here Nietzsche seems very individualistic; there must also be room for a less anti-social view of life, which stresses rather the extent to which we have successfully co-operated to develop a world of public meanings and shared interpretations.

(e) *Spoken by language*. Let's try then to put first, not the individual subject's will to power, but the common world of language. For it is language that alone gives us the classifications by which we order our world. We see the world in terms of our nouns and adjectives and prepositions, we see activities and processes in terms of verbs and adverbs. We learn to think the world and to act in it only as we are inducted into a world of language and language games that is always pre-existent. It is not just that language has its own rules that we happen to be unable to opt out of; the point is rather that we are constituted within the rules, and exist only in this framework, so that there is no sense in the notion of opting out. Language goes through our heads from ear to ear. We have no non-linguistic private thoughts. And it is not just that our Western metaphysics as laid down by Plato and Aristotle happens to look rather like the grammar of our Western languages; the point is rather that our language is inescapably and necessarily our metaphysics. Being language-shaped, our minds impose our grammar upon the world. That is why all facts are sentence-shaped: haven't you noticed?

Many people still find the point here hard to grasp. Try this: how could there be in the mind a bit of knowledge, or a formulated intention, or a meaningful claim, except in a sentence-ish shape? You disagree? – then kindly state your disagreement in some medium other than language in order to make yourself clear. You might, for example, express yourself by pointing to this page, grimacing, and hurling this book across the room – but your action will still presuppose some sentences, like this one, to explain it and to set it in relation to my other sentences.

Now we can state the three main doctrines of structuralism. First, setting aside inconsequential bits of animal behaviour, reflexes and so forth, every single human act is significant, that is, symbolic and communicative and so, in a broad sense at least, linguistic. Secondly, the code always precedes the sender and her particular message. Meaningfulness is not possible unless the code is already established and in place. Thirdly, the code has at least theoretically anticipated every message that can be sent in it.

Add to these three doctrines a number of psychological points. Verbal automatisms, post-hypnotic suggestion, puns and *doubles entendres*, dream-symbolism and other psychological phenomena appear to show at the very least that there is a great deal more linguistic activity going on inside us than we are aware of. People may, for example, be influenced for life by language that was graven on them before they could speak and of which they remain unconscious. What we find ourselves saying is a cut-down and drastically disciplined selection, made we don't quite know how, from a much larger and less disciplined background. Look into your own thoughts, and what do you find there but an ant-heap of part-formed sentences scurrying about in the semi-darkness? That noble thing they call the human mind is just language itself, teeming and seething inside our poor brains.

That we are 'spoken by language' is then not arrant nonsense but an epigrammatic way of saying that particular utterances like the sentences I am presently writing are produced from and within and according to the mysterious rules of a much larger and controlling background in the unconscious, in language games, in the Symbolic Order, in culture. And the upshot of all this is a quietistic and conservative account of our human condition. We cannot dislodge or escape from the sovereignty of 'the Law', as Lacan calls it.

(*f*) *History is over*. Once upon a time money was real wealth, gold and silver. The pound coin was a pound's worth of gold: economic realism. But in due course, first the 'real' coin was replaced by a printed paper pledge, and then money began to get more and more abstract and unreal as it took off into a world of its own. Financiers buy and sell money. Even odder, people deal in financial 'futures'.

What happened to money has happened also to language and the representation of reality. At some moment in the past economic development began to be led by consumption rather than by the productive process. The Romantic movement prepared the way for this by encouraging consumers to take a very great interest in their own feelings and to believe that they should pursue personal fulfilment by gratifying their desires. Romanticism was the child of Lutheranism because it was subjectively antinomian: within your inner life you were liberated from bondage to the law. You could even, in a way, *indulge* yourself. You should examine, explore, express, get to know, your own feelings. So Romanticism in turn became the mother of consumerism. The Romantic movement usefully demonstrated that it was possible to invent and to diffuse new feelings, like the feeling of being pleasurably frightened. Gothick shockers and suchlike could then be marketed in order to gratify these new feelings. The novel was one of the first products to be psychologically tailored to a particular market. But as consumption thus began to lead the economy the entire ideological superstructure became steadily less concerned with representing the real, and steadily more slewed towards creating ever-new desires and fantasies and attaching them to products. Images began to precede reality.

In our own time, the argument continues, 'postmodernism' is a term that designates the outcome of this process. In the type of society variously described as late-capitalist or post-industrial, the media and 'the market' dominate everything. We are immobilized in a state of ceaseless innovation. The dream-machine some time ago lost all touch with reality and escaped into fantasy. The real has progressively disappeared and has been replaced by media hyper-reality, an *ecstatic* form of reality, realer than reality. History vanishes into the news media which continuously scatter and forget it, and the human self is similarly sucked in and lost. We have now reached the condition which a number of science-fiction writers have been prophesying for about forty years. Everything is disappearing except the floating sign, the infinitely-seductive play of appearances, the flux of fashion, the dream of desire.

Six theories of our human condition then, which have been seriously put forward by figures of note. To recapitulate, we have been seen as:

      (*a*)   spirits trapped in the wrong world
      (*b*)   creatures in a cosmos
      (*c*)   spectators of a machine
      (*d*)   agents in the Void
      (*e*)   spoken by language
and as (*f*)   beings whose history is over.

All these views have been held, and they are only a small selection from a much larger number that could easily have been found and quoted – which reminds us again of the devastatingly nihilistic observation, made so casually, that every philosophical position tends to get taken. Doesn't that imply that almost anything can be made plausible, almost anything might be so, and that our theories are something like expressions of the market niche we've been jostled into by the struggle to make and sell a product of our own? Perhaps our theories only express our point of view, our psychological type and our spiritual biography? It seems that our human condition is so complex or so malleable that (as in biology) the struggle for literary existence can generate a great variety of life-forms. The greater the philosophical competition, the more exotic blooms appear. And that there is in the end no very sharp distinction here between truth and fiction is further suggested by the way the range of world-views to be found among great philosophers and theorists is not noticeably less wide than the range of outlooks to be found in imaginative literature generally. All the rigour, the high pretensions and the straining after Truth have done little to narrow the field: what can be held to be really so seems to remain almost as diverse as what can be imagined. We are still in the position Kant complained about and tried to remedy. Logic, mathematics and some areas of hard abstract philosophy are in fairly good order intellectually and can be distinguished from fictions, but concrete philosophy, philosophy of the human condition – that is, metaphysics and the philosophical appraisal of politics, ethics, art, religion and so forth – all *that* is in a very different case. Compare what is to be found in the two vast literary genres, philosophy and imaginative writing: does all this work justify a clear contrast between metaphysical truth and imaginative truth, between philosophy-truth and art-truth? It does not.

What sort of object then is a representation of the human condition in a text, whether literary, philosophical or religious? First, there is no one thing called 'the human condition'. There is no extra-historical and unchanging human nature. Around the world human lives at different times and places have been construed and constructed in very varied ways, and no one way is perennially compulsory. Rather, a text is an invitation to us to view life under certain images, and perhaps recommends us to live by them. Like a caricature, the text selects and exaggerates in a pleasurably illuminating way that also contrives to suggest evaluations. If there have already been sentences running through me to the effect that I am dissatisfied with my body and ill-at-ease in the world, then teachings to the effect that I am really a spirit and only briefly trapped in this body and this world will give me a buzz. It will ring true to me and suggest, perhaps, a programme of action. If on the other hand I am a disillusioned former marxist who feels defeated by the surreal, manipulative yet dissociated world of consumerism and television advertisements, then I will be impressed by Baudrillard's theory that in late capitalism there is no longer any point in theory, because 'the disappearance of the real' takes away with it all agents, action and history. The world has become a mad blare of publicity with no public. Yes, come to think of it, the ads certainly do prompt that thought. Today all philosophies, religions and life-views have themselves become just fads that we get *into*, that we go through, and that can touch us only aesthetically. Fictionalism.

Look again down that list of views of the human condition. The last three, and more recent, views are better able to account for the diversity of the list itself, because they stress creativity and plurality. Descartes (c) is a transitional figure, keen to maintain what he can of the older outlook, and especially the older dogmatic conception of Truth. Truth aestheticized, art-truth, manufactured truth, arrives in a big way only after Nietzsche. But then, after Nietzsche, what happens to the culture? Is there not a disturbing parallel between the development of philosophy and that of painting? The pace accelerates, and styles succeed one another with more and more rapidity. Diversification, fragmentation, dissolution. The growth in our ability to comprehend all previous styles is paralleled by a matching decline in our ability to make and be convinced by anything coherent of our own.

4. *What then is truth?*

Truth is just the property of being true, but it is also one of those cases where an adjective tends to develop a portentous cognate abstract noun – a case indeed like that of 'good' and 'evil', where the abstract nouns have similarly come to be thought of as standing for invisible essences whose nature we probe and about which we have theories. We assume that an abstract noun is a window upon an unchanging intelligible entity, a *thing* that the word designates. The word 'truth' stands for *the* Truth. Following Socrates, then, philosophy tries to descry and delineate this great and mysterious object, in the belief that if only we have our terms defined sufficiently clearly we won't make mistakes, and will be able to resolve our disagreements.

Since we have thought like this for thousands of years, it is hardly surprising that without a conscious effort to correct ourselves we just go on thinking in the old way. Yet the doctrine of capital-T Truth, Truth as an objective and unchanging essence out there, becomes quite implausible if we but pause a while to consider the widely-varying ways and contexts in which the word is used. Take the following five sorts of possibly-true statement:

Evaluations. Value-judgments, moral and aesthetic, have the grammatical form of descriptive assertions. Certainly many people who make them believe that what they are saying is true. Yet if value-judgments really are uncomplicatedly descriptive, why is it so difficult to reach general agreement about them? We cannot even agree about whether values are indeed mind-independent things out there, quasi-factually present or absent, in such a way that statements about their presence or absence *can* be quasi-factually true. An alternative theory maintains that value-judgments are expressive declarations of commitment in which we seek to persuade others to agree with us. But whatever view be taken, it is surely clear that there is something special and rather odd about the truth-status of evaluative judgments.

The a priori. A priori truth is truth in the fields of logic and mathematics. Here the nature of truth is again disputed: is *a priori* truth (*a*) out there in a strong sense, for example by being vested in the Divine Intellect, as rationalist metaphysics has claimed; or (*b*) genuinely and timelessly thought-constraining and to that extent at least mind-independent, but without needing to be either grounded or objectified metaphysically; or (c) just humanly-devised and conventional? We take the third of these views, pointing out that mathematical intuitions which have seemed self-evident in one period have been doubted in another. That is, the feeling of necessity is itself socially and historically produced, and changeable. But in any case, although the *nature* of *a priori* truth is disputed, its *criterion* is generally agreed to be consistency with the initially-agreed axioms and rules of inference. And consistency can probably be given a linguistic definition in terms of whether or not a sentence or chain of sentences can be read as well-formed and as performing a single intelligible speech-act, complex maybe, but at least not self-subverting. Often the issue is hard to decide, but formal systems try to make it as decidable as possible.

Metaphors and literal truth. Talk of truth is very often linked with literalism, the doctrine that sentences can exactly copy the shapes of facts. The *Oxford English Dictionary* entry on truth shows how profoundly the English language is imbued with literalism and the correspondence theory of truth. The definition of truth has depended upon the opposition between the literal and the metaphorical. However, those who know their Jacques Derrida will not fail to observe that *literalism itself consists in a whole fistful of metaphors*, metaphors of agreement, accord, copying, tracing, representing, picturing, matching, corresponding and so forth. 'Literalism' is a metaphor, 'metaphor' is a metaphor, and the 'transcendence' of metaphor is yet another metaphor. And the more Derrida and others compel us to recognize the rhetorical character of philosophical writing and the figurative or symbolic character of all languages, the more elusive the question of truth becomes.[6]

Stating facts. The standard case of a true-or-false assertion has traditionally been a fact-stating one. But what *is* a fact? Are there facts out there, or do facts only show themselves in the light of practical interests, cultural perspectives and theories? On this latter view there are facts for you only because you are a living, active, needy being with an interest in singling them out. Truth for you, then, is what you want to know. It is subjective and perspectival, but our common human needs and our conversation may nevertheless generate common (pragmatic) truths about a common human world.

Narrative truth. Witnesses in lawcourts, journalists and historians are much concerned with relating stories about events in the human world. The narrative form goes all the way down: I mean, the human world emerges in and through our telling and retelling of stories about it.[7] Trace all the way back the story of a news story: even before the bullet was ever fired, the murder was already a scheduled episode in a story, a story about his own grievances and intentions that the murderer was telling himself. Now follow the superimposition of various stories told from various angles during the next few hours, and one can begin to view the human world as an enormous struggling swarm of stories, competing, complementing, embroidering, corroborating and contradicting each other. Truth? – the story that comes out on top. And what *is* story-truth? Ah . . .

Here then are five regions where questions of truth arise with great urgency but are in varying ways obscure or difficult. Other areas could also have been mentioned, but these five are different enough from each other to make our present point.

In the past people's presumption in favour of unity, totality and system often led them to think that our life must make sense. There are no ultimate contradictions. In the end all truth is One. Everything adds up. To give expression to this idea, they would take whatever regional notion of truth appealed most to them and try to stretch it a bit so that it would cover everything. Rationalist metaphysics, for example, was most impressed by *a priori* truth, and believed that (at least in God's absolute and perspectiveless vision) the whole world and all Truth about it could be seen to have the unity and the satisfyingly self-evident necessity and consistency of a formal system. The coherence theory of truth amounted to the claim that the Whole Truth about the Universe could in principle be expressed in one extremely long but perfectly-formed and necessarily-true sentence.

By contrast, empiricists have held that all the truths about the world could in principle be captured in a very large number of very short sentences. Each sentence would record one contingent fact. Each fact is logically independent of every other fact, so no sentence would contradict any other. Thus empiricism typically favours a form of correspondence theory of truth. To make this scheme of thought work, it has to be supposed that we can check in each case the correspondence between simple sentence and simple fact. That means we need a method of getting hold of those simple facts which is theory-neutral and independent of language. The empiricists believed that sense-experience was the answer. They maintained, or assumed, that our sense-experience could be 'pure' and not conditioned by language and culture and history. So sense-experience gave direct access to facts, and made it possible directly to check whether the facts were getting portrayed accurately in the sentences. Or so it was thought.

Neither of these theories of truth is in the least persuasive today, but the pragmatist theory of truth, of which we have already given a hint, marks a real advance. It is functionalist in that it tries to acknowledge that the true for us has to be what it is good for us to hold, and it suits a period of rapid change because it allows us to think that beliefs and truths may have only a limited period of serviceability. We should regard our beliefs as being like disposable tools, and simply pick up the ones that will best serve our current purposes. From this angle, we might claim that religious beliefs are true in the sense that they work out well in our lives – and no more than that can be said or need be said, for we have no standpoint outside our own lives from which to conduct any other test of our beliefs.

But with pragmatism we have already come to the end of Truth, truth as One, truth as an unchanging intelligible essence. The old, strong idea of Truth – metaphysical, categorical, absolute truth – is usable only in the context of metaphysical realism and a cosmology. If there is a cosmos out there, if there is an objective intelligible order out there and independent of our discourse, then of course there is Truth out there. An objective intelligible order makes Truth seem natural, part of the constitution of the extra-human world.

However, when we looked 'locally' at truth we found it to be highly regional, variegated, human, disputed. Truth is human, socially-produced, historically-developed, plural and changing. We may make some progress by working at the various local uses of 'truth', but big, global capital-T Truth is a myth, and we would do well to give up talking about it, because there is nothing interesting to be said about it. Capital-T Truth is dead.

5. A question of order

The philosopher George Berkeley (1685–1753) was commonly believed to have denied the existence of matter. He himself called his doctrine 'immaterialism'. Others saw him as a subjective or (Kant's term) 'dogmatic' idealist – one who was sure only of the self, and regarded the external world as imaginary. Berkeley's views were attributed to insanity by some and to his Irishness by others. Dr Samuel Johnson kicked a stone, saying, 'I refute him thus!' Dean Swift allegedly refused to open his front door to admit Berkeley, saying that the philosopher should be as well able to walk through a closed door as an open one.

All philosophers are misunderstood, but Berkeley could fairly claim to have been more badly treated than most. His declared aim had been only that of 'recalling Men to Common Sense' (*Philosophical Commentaries*, §751). Why was he so misrepresented by otherwise intelligent people?

The answer is surely that in the past philosophers have often represented themselves as giving an inventory of the contents of the world; putting some things on the list and leaving others out, proving the existence of this and denying the existence of that. That makes it sound as if what is at stake is something factual, as if Berkeley's denial of the existence of matter were a claim that might indeed be demolished merely by finding, or just kicking, some material object. So a double absurdity arises: Berkeley has used language provocatively and given the impression that he thinks there are no physical things, and Samuel Johnson, rising to the bait, has ridiculed Berkeley for being so stupid as to have lived in this world for fifty years and more without ever noticing that there are rocks about the place.

To this day philosophers continue to put forward hyperbolical claims by way of attracting attention to their doctrines, as when Barthes denies the self, Foucault proclaims the death of man, and Baudrillard says that history is over. In each case a Samuel-Johnson type of reply is obviously possible: Barthes' books are after all written in a highly individual personal style, human beings are still alive and kicking, and history goes on. But it would be more sensible to regard the philosopher as urging the advantages of adopting a certain starting-point, a certain order of exposition, a certain group of metaphors, certain idioms and ways of speaking, so as to get the best angle on some current problem. Philosophy isn't about demonstrating that some things don't exist and others do; it's about getting into a better working order all the things we already know. There is only the human world, which is the world of language. Nothing is hidden, and philosophy is never going to find out anything that is not already plain to view in well-made and appropriately-used English sentences. There is nothing extra to be discovered. The problem is only to re-order, or to get the most useful and productive angle on, things that people are saying every day about minds, thoughts, words, experiences, values, actions, bodies and so on.

The classic case of all this is the mind-body problem. René Descartes suggested that the primary certainty which modern philosophy should begin from is to be found within individual subjectivity. I can doubt all else, but I cannot doubt my own existence as a thinking thing. An 'I'-philosophy of this sort next needs to explain how we move out of the inner private world of the self into the external public world. It has to be shown how we can get into objectivity, recognize other selves, enter into communication with them and establish a common human world.

Berkeley stands firmly in the tradition of Descartes, but he is also a British Empiricist who hopes he can improve a bit on the Cartesian starting-point. For Berkeley the minimal, primitive situation from which philosophy must start is not just I-think-therefore-I-am, but a *perceptual* situation. A perception is presented to a perceiver. So the world already contains two kinds of entity, perceivers and things-perceived, minds and presentations, knowing subjects and objects known, spirits and ideas. The objective world is then to be constructed by us out of our sensory input.

Berkeley thus has from the outset a little more objectivity in his system than Descartes had. But he still has problems, for if, for any object known, *X is real = X is perceived*, then we can never have any ground for saying either that anything is any more than the sum of its perceptible qualities or that these perceptible qualities can exist anywhere except 'in the mind' – that is, as objects of experience. If by 'matter' is meant imperceptible stuff out there and not in relation to any mind, then it is an idea we can never justify and do not need. And this makes Berkeley look as if he really is stuck in subjectivity. How on his account do we ever manage to establish a common public world?

Berkeley recognizes that in order to meet this point we must be able to distinguish between those of our experiences which are personal and relatively wild or wilful (such as dreams, fantasies and imaginings) and those of our experiences which seem to be willy-nilly *presented* to us and are forceful, stable and intersubjectively coherent. This latter class of experiences, the experiences we have of our common world, he thinks of as given to us by God's creative thought. Furthermore, God keeps it all going even when we are not adverting to it. So God is the universal fallback Perceiver who joins up the common world, gives it 'objectivity' and makes it reliably coherent. But there still isn't matter, even for God, if by 'matter' is meant imperceptible stuff not in relation to any mind. Material objects or physical things will have to be analysed as clumps of sense-experiences. And this doctrine is by no means as silly as Johnson and Swift appear to have thought. In its defence we can at least point out that you cannot refute the claim that matter is reducible to experiences merely by citing against it *experiences*, such as those of kicking stones and walking into doors.

Berkeley is not out of the wood yet, though. For one thing, if I can never be justified in postulating 'matter' as an imperceptible stuff out on the far side of the screen of my experiences, how can I be justified in postulating an imperceptible thing called your mind, out on the far side of that cluster of my experiences that I call your body? But we need not go into more detail: everyone knows by now that any philosophy that starts within the sphere of individual subjectivity has problems in getting out into language, society and the external world.

In a situation like this creative philosophy attempts to change the angle of vision, to start in a different place or to reverse the order of the argument. Starting in subjectivity, Berkeley cannot entirely satisfactorily make the move out into objectivity. So let us quote the appropriate Irishism at him: 'If I were trying to get to where you're trying to go, I wouldn't be starting from here. Let's set off from a different place.' Instead of beginning with the private and struggling to get from there to the public, let's try starting with the public and treating the private as, not basic, but derivative. Let's begin with the common language and treat thought as internalized speech, instead of treating speech as a merely secondary device for exteriorizing and transmitting thought. Instead of seeing society as constructed by individuals, let's see the individual as a sort of human being that has been produced for its own purposes by a certain kind of society. Let's see linguistic meaning as produced by a public consensus about usage, rather than as being injected into words *ad hoc* by private acts of intending.

This particular reversal is philosophically extraordinarily powerful; but it is also extraordinarily difficult to persuade people fully to move over to the new order of exposition. If it is going to change anything, philosophy is going to have to get up to some very heavy rhetorical tricks. Among them 'denying the existence' of the soul or the mind is almost bound to figure. If we 'deny the existence of the mind', we seem to be making a rather extravagant assertion in dogmatic metaphysics. Gilbert Ryle's *The Concept of Mind* (1949) was understood in this way, and people mocked a philosopher who 'proclaimed that men were all bodies/ while holding a Chair at All Souls'. But on the interpretation I am proposing, a bold metaphysical assertion is a rhetorical device used in the hope of persuading people to change the habitual order of their thoughts. Berkeley reversed against the Newtonians and 'denied the existence of matter'; Ryle reversed against the Descartes-Berkeley tradition and 'denied the existence of minds'. Each move was highly pertinent and illuminating in its day. As for the Truth – forget it. Philosophy is occasional. At different times different strategies are opportune.

What used to be called 'reductionism' was a way of emphasizing the importance of the order of treatment. Thus Berkeley himself grew up at a time when Newton's physics and Locke's philosophy had between them contrived to get the whole question of 'the external world' and our knowledge of it into a tangle. The Newtonians seemed to be saying that the abstract mathematized world of physics, made only of matter in motion and having only the so-called 'primary qualities', was the Real world behind the veil of sense. This was dogmatic Platonism with a vengeance: it put the physicist in the seat of the metaphysician and the theologian. It said that whereas ordinary folk see only flickering shadows, the scientist enjoys something like privileged knowledge of the world that Really Is. But this new edition of Plato's Intelligible World is very bleak, being made *only* of material bodies moving about in space and time according to mathematical laws. Berkeley the churchman saw very clearly what would follow: dogmatic atheism and an all-out metaphysical materialism that would reduce 'Common Sense', the ordinary person's vision of the life-world, to a misleading appearance.

To put things right Berkeley needs a clear distinction between physics and metaphysics, so that physical science can be told to be just science, and be stopped from getting too big for its boots by claiming strong Philosophical knowledge of the world. Berkeley needs that distinction, but in his day it was not available. The term

Natural Philosophy covered both physics and metaphysics. Indeed, that was precisely the trouble: Berkeley's age lacked a critical philosophy of science that, by questioning the status of scientific knowledge, would help to dissuade people from understanding it in an unduly inflated dogmatic or metaphysical sense.

Berkeley's solution is to change the order. He argues that instead of seeing the world of physical theory as primary and then treating the world of Common Sense as a half-illusory effect produced by it upon our sense organs, we would do better to see the world of Common Sense as primary and then treat the world of physical theory as a collection of useful man-made fictions and mathematical rules for solving various problems. So Berkeley seeks to demolish the grand metaphysical pretensions of Newtonianism, without denying in the least its utility just as science; and he aims in the process to kick out metaphysical capital-M Matter as the substrate behind the world of experience, and to bring back God. Unfortunately Berkeley failed, for he did not prevent metaphysical materialism (and therefore atheism) from developing during his own lifetime, among the French *avant-garde* in particular. And perhaps one reason for his failure was that, given the limitations of what was available to him at that time, he had to cast his project in the form of a virtuoso exercise in reductionism. His rhetorical strategy had to take the form of pretending to out-Locke Locke, by being more consistent and thoroughgoing in his Cartesianism and his empiricism than Locke had been. So Berkeley begins with spirits, or perceivers, and ideas, or things perceived, and attempts to annihilate metaphysical materialism by showing that our world is made *only* of ideas or experiences. He did rather well; but given the intellectual and spiritual crisis of his time, and given the resources and devices available to him, he had to employ a reductionist strategy which produced a result that seemed too implausible. So he was mocked by people such as Swift and Johnson, who should have been his allies. To a modern reader it looks as if Berkeley has expressed himself with the very greatest eloquence and clarity. It would seem to be just about impossible to mistake his meaning, and yet everyone did mistake it. Just about everyone, that is, except (by a strong and sweet irony) a second, New-World, Samuel Johnson from Stratford, Connecticut.

As we have seen, Berkeley reversed against a kind of meta-physical materialism that made Matter into a Thing-in-Itself transcending experience. Berkeley hated the thought that Matter should come first in this way. If Matter were allowed to retain that kind of primacy it would wipe out God, and unbelieving natural philosophers, or 'physicists' as they would one day come to be called, would replace theologians and philosophers as the chief authorities in the culture. To dethrone Matter Berkeley re-called his contemporaries to the teaching of Descartes and Locke, that in our scientific age philosophy must begin with the thinking subject and with experience. Berkeley's cunning was to argue that if people were fully consistent in adhering to the Cartesian-empiricist starting-point and method, then Matter as a meta-physical, explanatory concept would be exposed as useless and illusory. And in a sense Berkeley was quite right. Indeed, his problem was that he was *too* right. He had taken a step backwards, behind his own retina, and the world was now only flickerings on the inner surface of his own sense-organs. His retina had become semi-opaque, and he was looking at it from behind. This certainly does get rid of Matter. Unfortunately it also gets rid of a lot else that is much more important than Matter, namely, the public world of linguistic meaning, human communication and human action.

So in due course there would have to be a complex reversal against Berkeley, a reversal that would establish the priority of the social and the public, of language and culture. A human being cannot think, cannot speak, cannot act in an intelligible way except within a culture and a language which are always already in place. There is a social *a priori* and it is transcendental, in the sense that it is always there, presupposed as a condition of the possibility of human life. We cannot function as human beings except in a vocabulary, given to us by society, which has been historically evolved and which is still changing. You don't exist as a person except as a product of culture and language, and as a period piece.

It is extraordinary that this idea should have emerged so recently and with such difficulty. Berkeley seems quite to lack it. Hume has an inkling of it, Hegel and Marx have more, French social theory states it clearly (in Durkheim and Lévy-Bruhl), and yet Wittgenstein's much-fought-over arguments against the possibility of a private language show how very recently it was *still* novel and controversial. The full implications emerge most clearly in post-War French thought. Freud and Marx find themselves getting rewritten in radically linguistic and structuralist terms respectively by Lacan and Althusser.[8] This opens the way to a whole series of interconnected reversals, as a result of which Culture gets put before Nature, superstructure before base, public before private, the social before the individual, vocabulary and structure before particular utterances and performances, and meaning before being. Thus far, the new doctrine of the priority of the public and the structural has had the air of a reaction against Sartre, who (like Ayer in England) was something of a late-Cartesian. Even Sartre himself felt constrained to qualify his own early individualism a little. But by the late 1960s it was beginning to be recognized that the doctrine that we are all of us programmed by language and other social structures was being used as an ideological defence of the necessity and inescapability of the modern bureaucratic state. How could one open a space for freedom and dissent, without going back to individualism? The answer was poststructuralism, with its sharp criticism of the metaphysical tradition and its dazzling new series of truly bewildering reversals. Difference precedes sameness, relations precede their terms, and so on.

Questions of order, then, are of very great importance in philosophy, and especially in recent philosophy. When, to solve a current problem, philosophy says that we must reverse the order so far and start taking B before A instead of after it, it always seems that the very existence of A is being denied. The logically-prior is taken to be the real, and the secondary seems to be demoted to non-existence. Often philosophers themselves are quite happy to put it that way, denying matter like Berkeley, or mind like Ryle. And suppose that a time comes when we want to reverse the order of treatment *all over the place*? Then the more complete the programme of reversal, the more comprehensive the denial of previously-accepted realities.

We live in a time when such a wholesale reversal is indeed taking place, and *that* is why we are talking about nihilism. For nihilism may be treated, not as if it were the Truth about things (namely, that there is no truth), now at last discovered, but rather as a special kind of mood or feeling produced by the removal of all landmarks in a period of very extensive cultural change.

Thus we can be nihilistic even about nihilism. We give up truth out-there, natural truth. We come to see the history of philosophy as a series of pendulum-swings, occasionally-called-for shifts in the order of exposition. And now nihilism itself becomes just another passing phase. Is this absurd? – but it is how we hear people speak every day about the gyrations of fashion in matters of truth, morality and belief.

6. *Realism and anti-realism*

The older sort of philosophy that Kant called 'dogmatic meta-physics' looked back in many ways to the natural philosophy of early presocratic times. It aimed to give a general theory of Reality as a whole. But the idea of Reality as a whole is in effect the idea of a cosmos. It supposes that there is a formed, systematically-unified and intelligible order of things out there, independent of and prior to the human thinking and language that then come along and try to re-present it. The Greeks were not keen to entertain the suggestion that we don't in fact have a cosmos at all. Formlessness was repugnant to them.

Yet if we do have a cosmos, why is the nature of Reality-as-a-whole not obvious to every one of us? Why should we need experts to tell us what it is, and why do the experts differ so much among themselves? So far as this question gets raised and answered at all, the answer seems to be that we mortals are fallen into a condition of alienation, ignorance and confusion, and the philosopher is a person who has struggled free by dint of superior ability, methods and training. The philosopher is an elect soul, purified to receive the Truth and qualified to teach it to us. And why is it so important for us to know it? Because that antecedent intelligible order of things is rather like religious Law (Torah, Ma'at, Dhamma, Tao). It is *authoritative*, and we need to conform our thought and practice to it if we are to get on the right lines.

In this way human knowledge was from the outset conceived of as (*i*) coming second, and (*ii*) copying or conforming itself to something that was prior, cosmic and normative. The philosopher was therefore committed to being a spokesman for a certain vision of the established order of things, defending its wisdom and goodness, teaching the Law and purveying authoritative knowledge. He was a little like a School Prefect, explaining the school's organization and rules to the wide-eyed new bugs, and impressing upon them the need to recognize their own proper place and be unobtrusively dutiful. (At my own school there was even an examination in all this lore.) And these new bugs must above all *fit in*.

We see here how closely inter-related are a whole family of ideas: realism, a cosmos, a creation-myth to be recited, and an ethic of discovering and then fitting into your assigned place in the cosmic scheme. Realism is highly political. Constantly re-affirmed on all sides, it inculcates an ethic of 'my station and its duties' such as is suitable for a well-ordered class society. Realism is cosmic Toryism.

Certainly there are several kinds of realism. By far the most significant is Plato's sort, namely belief in the real and objective existence of the Forms in the noumenal world. This was a realism or objectivism about meanings, essences, intellectual objects, standards of thought and value. The claim is that my knowledge-claims and my evaluations, to be right, must meet absolute and unchanging cosmic standards. When the standards are met the mind and the world, language and reality, fit each other perfectly.

Plato's presumption is that the way the Greek language, correctly used, currently carves up Reality is the way Reality itself divides up.

Plato's extreme linguistic supernaturalism has some more recent parallels. In 1980 a work of Arabic philology was suppressed in Egypt because it appeared to suggest that the Arabic language is human and has evolved historically, whereas in reality, as we know, the Qu'ran pre-existed from all eternity in the divine mind *in Arabic*. Thus strong realism about our standards of thought and value, about religious truth and the meanings of words, calls for a supernaturalism of language with two main themes in it: first, there is a pre-established and finalistic reciprocal accord between language and reality, and secondly, since the cosmic order (at least, at the top level) is pre-established and unchanging, language must be so too.

Most people still think all this. For them words are transparent and open directly on to unchanging objective meanings or essences. These essences that they are about give words reference and hold them still. To most people the idea that a natural language is only a shifting human improvisation, with nothing to guarantee its agreement with reality, is unbearably sceptical in its implications.

Plato's kind of realism is evidently religious (at least, insofar as one accepts the typically Western understanding of religion as acceptance, pious self-subordination and service), and it is noteworthy that the teacher to whom Plato gives the highest rank is the intellectual contemplative.

As for the world of sense-experience, Plato takes a rather non-realist view of it. Since the Forms do not and cannot become properly incarnated in it, the phenomenal world is a mere realm of shadows, a flux of appearances. It does not have enough stable or determinate structure to be either real or knowable. And this vision of the sensible world keeps threatening to return as 'phenomenalism' in post-Cartesian empiricist philosophy, in Berkeley, Hume, Mill, Russell and others. For these writers realism is usually not a doctrine about the status of the Forms, but rather an affirmation of the reality of 'the external world', on the far side of the screen of sense-experience. From this point of view the people with a reassuringly strong conviction that we are not hallucinating, and that there is a real physical world out there, are figures like Aristotle, Thomas Reid and G. E. Moore.

However, although it has been much debated, the question of the reality of the external world is not so very important. Whether you follow Berkeley or Aristotle, as Berkeley himself remarks, 'the horse is in the stable, the Books are in the study as before'.[9] The difference, as we have seen, lies only in the order of exposition, and in what for a particular age is an appropriate philosophical strategy. It is not an empirical difference and, as Berkeley again insists, 'the Vulgar' need not be troubled about it. Far more important is the realism that maintains that truth is truly given to us or discovered by us and *not* just made by us; the realism that affirms Truth out there, Meanings out there, moral standards out there, a perspectiveless, authoritative, unifying, complete account of things out there. As we suggested, it is politically conservative, and pictures the universe as being rather like an English boarding school. You should accommodate yourself or fit yourself into a pre-established guiding order of things. Knowledge (*i*) came second, and (*ii*) copied intelligible reality. In view of all this, it is not surprising that Kant, at the height of the Enlightenment and teaching that human beings had now at last come of age, should have set out to reverse the old assumptions. In his Critical Philosophy (*i*) knowledge comes first, and (*ii*) reality must conform itself to our knowledge. There is no longer a match or correspondence between two things, our knowledge and the way things are. There is only one thing, namely reality-fixed-in-knowledge. What the physical universe is for us depends upon and is determined by the current state of our physical sciences and by our view as to the status of scientific knowledge. I look up into the sky, and current astronomical theory determines what I see. I see, for example, empty space and not blue glass. Theory shapes perception. Reality doesn't come first and then get itself copied by our knowledge; rather, reality becomes itself for us in our knowledge of it.

Kant described his own position in the formula, 'empirical realism and transcendental idealism'. The raw data of experience were genuinely given to us, as if from outside. But also, although Kant had transformed Plato's real order of eternal, intelligible Forms out-there into an ideal order of *a priori* concepts in our heads, he had of course most emphatically retained the necessity of those concepts. His brilliant insight, learned from the shock that Hume had given him, was that realism or objectivity *depends upon necessity*. That is, necessarily-true principles are needed in order to convert our merely subjective seemings into genuinely objective knowledge. These principles describe the basic structure that any objective and knowable world must have. If they can be proved, they will get us out of mere subjectivity.

Kant, as we said, has given up the idea of correspondence. We cannot institute a direct comparison between the thing in representation and the thing as it is in itself. We cannot step right out of our own point of view to check the objective well-foundedness of our perspectival representations. But Kant grasps that we are still entitled to call ourselves realists if and only if we can prove that we don't just happen to construct the world in the way we do, but *must* so construct it. What makes the world of experience real is the fact that raw data were presented to us, and the framework into which we fitted them was a framework of *a priori* necessary truths whose validity did not depend upon our will, nor upon anything empirical. Kant calls these truths 'synthetic a priori judgments', and for him realism or objectivity depends upon them, simply because they are the necessary conditions for there ever being any objective empirical knowledge of a world by a finite knower.

So the data were given, and the framework was compulsory; and that is realism or objectivity established from within, and not depending *either* upon any dubious ideas of correspondence *or* upon there being an absolute vision of the world against which our partial visions can be checked.

Kant's account is undoubtedly superior to its rivals. Consider some of the extra-Kantian arguments for realism. (1) From

Descartes and Locke: I seem to have experience of an objective world, I know God has the power to create such a world, and I know God is not a deceiver; therefore it is reasonable to believe that there *is* such a world. (2) A real material world transcending our experience is needed to be the cause of our experience. (3) A real world out-there must be postulated to account for the stability and the coherence of the world, both in relation to our different senses, and in relation to different human subjects. (4) From Husserl and Sartre: consciousness is always transitive or intentional; that is, it is always consciousness-of, so that to be itself it must always already have a real object. The very existence of *le pour-soi* presupposes *l'en soi*.

The weakness of these arguments is that even Berkeley can easily meet all of them. In Berkeley's system the job which the arguments claim only a real material world out there can do for us is done – and, Berkeley claims, done a whole lot better – by God. For, says Berkeley, since God is a spirit and has causal power, I can perhaps understand how God could cause me to have my experiences, whereas we have no idea of how inert matter could ever give rise to our rich and varied sense-experience. There is also a modern American version of Berkeley's challenge, in the question: 'How do I know I'm not a brain in a vat?' Here a computer takes the place of God. A brain kept alive in a glass vat is wired to the computer, which sends electrical impulses down the brain's sensory nerves, all in such a way that everything is exactly as if the brain were that of a complete human being living the same life as you are living. Now how do you know you are not yourself a brain in a vat like that? Since the computer, and, even more, the God of Berkeley, is able to supply everything that a real-world-out-there was thought to supply, the four arguments so far considered are insufficient.[10]

There is a final argument of sorts, (5) From Hume, and perhaps Wittgenstein: objectivity is a natural belief which we don't have sufficient reason to give up, and indeed which nobody can in practice consistently renounce anyway. But this is more an expression of weariness than an argument.

So Kant continues to seem stronger than his rivals. He grasped more clearly than anyone else that if objectivity is to be established at all it must be established immanently, and that the only way this could be done would be by a transcendental proof that we don't just happen to conceive the world in the way we do, but *must* so conceive it – at least in its most general structural features.

So far so good. The weakness of Kant's case shows negatively in what has been left out of the *Critique of Pure Reason*. Kant takes a strangely supernaturalist view (as he must) of necessity and of his own arsenal of concepts. He does not discuss the dependence of thought upon language, the diversity of natural languages, or the nature of linguistic meaning and its relation to long-term cultural change. Extremely logicist, he has nothing to say about the more rhetorical and literary uses of language. He is preoccupied with vindicating Newtonian physics, and does not discuss our knowledge of other human beings. In short, Kant's argument owes much of its plausibility to his omission of all the considerations to do with the contingency of language and culture and the historicality of human life that have come to the fore since his time.

Briefly, then, some arguments against realism: (1) Kant is right in saying that to establish the truth of realism we would need to establish objective or absolute necessity in at least some of the principles that guide our construction of our world. But such necessity is not forthcoming. Everything depends on language, and language is all contingent. Necessity is only conventional, and conventions can and do change. There are many ways of worldmaking, and the end of Newton's hegemony has already, and ironically, relativized a good deal of Kant's own argument, much that Kant thought logically necessary having already turned out not to *happen* to be so. (2) We have no sufficient reason to believe that one of the natural languages, at some particular stage in its historical development, has suddenly clicked, or even could suddenly click, into precise structural isomorphism with Reality. Unless that were to happen, the realistic vision could never get articulated. But what would it be for it to happen, and how would we be able to tell that it had happened? (3) For realism to be true there must be a way things really are that is at last articulable in language. But Final Truth is never reached, because the nature of language is such that there is no sentence whose meaning and interpretation are so clear as to be beyond any possibility of further dispute. The consequence is that reality never gets fully closed or fixed, but goes on being contested endlessly. The world is an argument that never gets settled. So there is no objectively-determinate real world that could ever be finally fixed in language.

7. The end of the problem of evil

A striking symptom of our new condition is the fading away of the problem of evil. Even as recently as a generation or two ago many people still asked after a major disaster, 'Why did God let it happen?' – as if they felt that it ought not to have happened, and as if therefore they felt they had a right to expect the way things go to be moral, and felt themselves to have been badly let down when it turned out not to be so. But why do we feel we have a right to expect things to be other than they are? In a striking short piece of 1973 the theologian John Robinson sharply rejected this version of the problem of evil.[11] One should not in any way invoke the 'categories of deliberation or purpose' in connection with the phenomena of Nature, 'nebulae, earthquakes, sunsets, cancers, tapeworms'; on the contrary, 'the meaninglessness, the literal senselessness of it all . . . is as much a part of the evolutionary process for the Christian as for the non-Christian'. Robinson insists: 'For the Christian no more than for anyone else is there purpose or intention in the ravages of a cancer.'

In Robinson's theology one should not say that God causes natural events, but rather that God is to be found in them. 'Love is there to be met, responded to *and created* through them and out of them.'[12] Robinson's language is notoriously vague and metaphorical, but he seems to be saying that religious faith overcomes the meaningless by a sort of expressive personalism which is determined in all situations to go on saying 'Yes' to the love of God, and which refuses to be beaten. Like Emil Fackenheim, Robinson is saying that faith's concepts can be imposed upon experience, even though they cannot be inferred from it. I refuse to allow evil people or tragic events to defeat my faith in God. I just insist on living my life *as if* it were a dialogue with a loving World-Ground, and in an ineffable way I feel vindicated. God is *a priori*, and so long as faith is also an *a priori* it cannot be defeated by facts. So perhaps Robinson was a theological non-realist: who is to say? The phrase *'and created'* (Robinson's own italics) implies a view of the type I have myself put forward, namely a thoroughly 'creationist' account of faith as an active making-sense of the senseless which either is its own reward, or hopes to be rewarded – maybe.

No matter: that is all by the way. What is really striking (and could not have been found in any period earlier than the late twentieth century) is such an open insistence on Nietzschean nihilism on the part of a bishop. There is no moral world-order out there, no great Purpose out there, no plan out there. '*We* invented the concept "purpose": in reality purpose is *lacking*.'[13] World events start to fall into storylike patterns only as we narrate them. All the time we are turning the world into language (or producing the world as language) and as we do so we supply the story, the purpose, and the moral values. We narrate the world, and in doing so we try to make it moral. There is no story out there: stories come only in language, and therefore can come only from us. It is a great relief to be able to say this, and to know that it has become obvious. We are delivered from having to try to make ourselves and others believe that the world makes sense by itself, that world-events all subserve one great moral purpose, that there is an aim or point to it all. Trying to keep those ideas going leads to a great deal of dishonesty and dissatisfaction. False expectations from life can only produce a factitious disappointment with life, which makes people miss out badly.

But if all this is right – and Robinson stuck to his position when, ten years later, he found that he himself had an inoperable cancer – then we really have come a very long way. For the assumption of many or most thinkers before World War II was that ordinary human beings would always find the thought of a random 'meaningless' universe, with nobody to blame and no ultimate explanation or remedy, to be utterly unendurable. Nietzsche thought that we would rather believe that our sufferings give pleasure to a sadistic God than accept that they are quite accidental, unnoticed and inconsequential. At any moment in our lives we may suddenly be overwhelmed by terrorism, personal catastrophe, madness, fatal illness, violence and sudden death. We all tread close to the brink, and eventually every one of us must topple over it. Bad news. So we invent various belief-systems in order to fend off the uncertainty and random violence of life, and make the universe appear more comfortingly solid and predictable than it is: we invent matter, physical laws, determinism, necessities and endless myths of special protection, as well as the mountain of social institutions that are designed to make life seem secure. Surely we wouldn't be so prolific in these inventions unless we were very, very frightened of life's sheer contingency?

So Nietzsche thought. Similar considerations were put forward by Evans-Pirtchard in *Witchcraft, Oracles and Magic Among the Azande* (1937), one of the most influential of all modern works in the human sciences. In my household, and doubtless also in yours, when something goes wrong or is found to be missing or broken the cry goes up. 'Who is to blame?' (It is usually me.) People need to know to what to attribute their particular misfortunes, and when the misfortune is really important it is not enough merely to quote to them some combination of natural causes, chance and perhaps their own carelessness. They want more than that. They want some sort of moral, social or religious – that is, in general terms, some sort of *personal* – explanation of why just this misfortune struck just them at just this moment. Religious professionals are expected to provide such explanations. And the vast proliferation of religious professionals, practices and ideologies bears eloquent witness to people's urgent need for intelligibility, for a recourse and for hope.

These human needs, according to Evans-Pritchard, are the key to understanding sin, sorcery and witchcraft. They provide various explanatory options: (*i*) misfortune may have struck because you or someone close to you has violated a prohibition, so that ritual impurity has been incurred. This in turn has attracted the wrath of God or of some lesser spirits. The diviner will explain the details and prescribe appropriate rituals to restore normality. Or (*ii*), sorcery may have been directed against you. A sorcerer is a sort of black-magic person, a professional man who can be hired and who uses 'medicines', so that sorcery is motivated and technically-directed maleficence. (*iii*) Alternatively, you may be the victim of witchcraft. Witchcraft is often conceived of as a substance present in some people's bodies that may operate without their being aware of it. The witch-doctor's diagnosis may make the witch conscious for the first time of his or her powers, and that can be dangerous.

Evans-Pritchard's discussion thus suggests a whole series of useful cognitive and social functions for witchcraft-belief. It explains misfortunes, providing an evil principle to account for them. Because witches are everything you should not be and do many things that you should never do, the image of the witch acts as a dire warning, and so functions as part of the system of social control. Making and following up charges of witchcraft provides a vocabulary in which to conduct quarrels, bringing them to a head and resolving them. Sometimes a witchhunt in society is cathartic, or may be the means by which social change takes place.

Among the Zande, the specialists summoned in case of sickness purport to take out of the victim's body various physical objects supposedly put into it by witches. Evidently they must remember to bring such objects along with them to the ritual. Does this mean that they must know, and the people must know, that they are 'really' charlatans? Evans-Pritchard allows that the Zande themselves may be sceptical about the genuineness of particular witchdoctors; but what matters most and what they cannot do without is the comforting explanatory value of witchcraft beliefs. It seems that there simply has got to be a 'morally' or 'personally' satisfying explanation of just why it has to be I who am suffering this now. Appeal to the operation of general laws is not sufficient. And no doubt in modern Western societies, in the public response to AIDS, in people's resort to mediums and clairvoyants, and in the quest of many ordinary individuals to make sense of their own lives, one can still find many survivals of these traditional ways of thinking.

Nietzsche and Evans-Pritchard appear then to be claiming that so far as the average human being is concerned, there's just got to be someone to blame. That is, whether it is 'objectively' illusory or not, there has to be some kind of social-moral explanation of the incidence of misfortune. People cannot live without meaning, 'meaning' meaning that somebody means me well or means me ill. And we might add that for the Zande there is not yet a problem of evil, because they find (or at least, they found) their traditional resources for explaining and coping with evil to be adequate. The same is doubtless true of large tracts of both biblical and mediaeval history. If belief in God is vigorous, if God is the cause of all events, if it is always right to turn to God and if people are confident that for each occasion in life they know both how to interpret it, and what the appropriate way of turning to God in that situation is – then indeed there *is* no problem of evil, because in every situation there is always a recourse, always, that is, some socio-moral explanation and something laid on that is relevant and good to be done. If you are hit hard, then God is punishing you for your sins, and we are all of us sinners, so it is always good to turn to God in contrition and plea for mercy. If you are sorely tried, then God is admonishing you or chastening you and you should pray to be preserved by him through the trials he is laying upon you. If you are richly blessed, you should praise and thank him. You are never at a loss, because the entire range of possible life-situations has a corresponding range of appropriate responses already prescribed within the religious system. Everything has been anticipated, so that when a religion is working well the problem of evil is not felt acutely. The practice of religion surmounts it daily.

The classical problem of evil arises when this ancient practical

and personalizing religious response to evil has been partly super-
seded by the development of a more regularized and naturalistic
picture of the world. From (roughly) Aristotle onwards philosophy develops the idea of a more or less autonomous order of
Nature governed by universal laws. We can all see why it is good
news that there is a real, stable cosmos, governed by knowable
and reliable laws. In such a world we are encouraged to be enquir-
ing and prudent, and are enabled to predict and plan ahead. The
world-order may now be traced back to the wise, regular Providence of God. As for the hard cases, their occasional occurrence is
surely a consequence of the general reliability which in other contexts we prize. Besides, we may well say to ourselves, in such hard
cases – which certainly occur – why may we not slip back to the
older tradition of an interventionist God? We can complain direct
to the Boss about the ways his own laws are working out . . .
can't we?

But now things begin to get very complicated. There is a certain conflict between the God of universal law and the God of
life's occasional ups and downs. Is the same God to be praised
regularly for being so perfectly regular, but also reproached now
and then when after all he turns out to be irregular? In any case,
consider a typical 'irregularity'. Human evolution (according to
present theory) could not have taken place within the set-up we've
got, unless the chromosomes were a little unstable. Things have
to be able to go a bit wrong so as to introduce variety. A consequence of this is that a proportion of human births are deformed.
Suppose *my* baby is born deformed. What then is my recourse?
The regular God says, 'Sorry, old thing, but it had to happen. I
can't break my own rules. Not your fault; just your bad luck.'
The archaic God says, 'Now will you repent, and turn to me
again?' And there is also the loving Father of Jesus Christ who
numbers the hairs of our heads. I plan to address my complaint to
the latter, but which complaint is it going to be – that his *ad hoc*
judgment was unjust and he should have intervened personally to
stop this thing from happening, or alternatively that with his
super-computer brain he ought to have been able to design the

whole set-up better in the first place? I don't know whether my misfortune was a punishment or an accident. Thus, as I say, things get complicated, and these complications generate the so-called 'problem of evil' because they give rise to conflicting views about what is an adequate and appropriate religious response to affliction.

The problem of evil is not that evils occur to us, but that we are unsure of the correct response – resignation, repentance, protest or whatever. The condition was common in late antiquity during the heyday of the popular cosmic religion and the Stoic natural theology, and it became common again in the Newtonian period, the two centuries after 1687. In both epochs religious uncertainty was generated by tension between a strong natural theology of cosmic order and perfection, and the sort of particularism that asks why God has chosen to do just this to me, just now. The former refuses the latter the kind of answer it seeks. The individual wants an ethical explanation *ad hominem*, but all he's allowed is an explanation in terms of general laws. If he insists on taking both, they will work against each other. He is in religious distress, because the prevailing religious system is not offering a consistent and clear way of coping with the contingencies of life.

All the more astounding, then, that since Darwin and Nietzsche so many people should so quickly have left all these ways of thinking behind. Although people still gather for memorial services and the like after a disaster, they do not ask why God let it happen, because they have in fact gone over to what by past standards is a radically atheistic and emotionally intolerable view of life. We've suddenly found that we can after all endure 'meaninglessness'. Our society in general accepts that there simply is not any satisfying religious-type answer to the question of why some are unexpectedly struck down, and not others. Insurance companies do very well on the assumption of randomness. In the generation around the age of twenty a certain proportion of young people get knocked out by spinal cancer, schizophrenia, travel accidents – and we no longer even so much as raise the traditional why-question. My religious friends, priests and theologians, nowadays actually prefer to accept like everyone else the unmotivated and arbitrary malignancy of life. One of them writes to say that he would rather think of his wife's recent terminal illness and death as a tragic accident than believe that a loving heavenly Father, for his own wise purposes, has chosen to do *that* to her. There is a certain decency about statistical misfortune, meaninglessness and the pathos of transience. We are all of us nihilists nowadays – at least, when we are thinking clearly. Even those who claim to be theological realists turn out in the event to regard their own faith as something that helps them to survive and surmount evil, rather than something that helps them to explain it. The problem of evil has come to an end because we no longer think we have a right to expect the way things go to be, by itself and apart from our efforts, a moral story. But I can still think of faith as binding me to do my bit to try to *make* the way things go into a moral story.

8. Speech, writing, absence

A number of distinct lines of argument now converge.

The last great generation of theistic philosophers was that of Berkeley, Leibniz and others at the beginning of the eighteenth century. For these writers the world cannot be merely the synthesis of our various human angles upon it. A central, unifying and absolute vision is needed as well, to hold everything together. It acts as a matrix. It grounds our various finite perspectives. It is the hub, the Centre, the coping-stone, the God's-eye-view. Without it the whole edifice of the world collapses into rubble. So God continued to be necessary to sustain the world and give it objectivity, until the Enlightenment was well under way. But then Hume in the early 1730s felt everything disintegrate. In response Kant made an immense effort to extract a shared, objective world just from within human subjectivity. He did not claim, in today's manner, to produce it from the social interactions of many finite human subjects: instead he claimed that objectivity was a transcendental condition of the possibility of there being *any* finite subject. Kant's valiant, extraordinary effort to prove objectivity by a new route shows that, Protestant though he was, he realized that God would not again ground the world and underwrite knowledge in quite the old way.

Since Kant the world has increasingly come to be seen as just the product of the interactions of a lot of finite human viewpoints. For social interactions generate meanings and therefore language, and therefore knowledge which is carried within language, and therefore the world which is produced within our knowledge (because we have no way of separating the way the world really is from the way it is presented within our own knowledge of it). So the world has gradually turned into a changing human cultural construction. We haven't got the world absolutely; we have only angles and perceptions. We can compare different human 'perceptions' of reality with each other, of course, but we cannot compare them with reality-as-such. Our new provisional language-generated world just isn't quite as real and solid as the old God-made Cosmos used to be. In fact it doesn't amount to much more than the-current-state-of-the-debate. The world is suspended within the evolving human argument. Our talk forms and calls forth its own subject-matter, or as the jargon has it, discourses produce their referents. Odd, disorienting, and (at first) easily misunderstood. But that is what we are now becoming accustomed to.

Secondly, a particularly striking indicator of all this is our recent tendency to refuse the problem of evil. It seems that we no longer expect the world to make sense antecedently and on its own account, before we come along to make sense of it. We no longer expect the world to have its own master-story about itself to tell, prior to and independently of the stories that we tell about it. We scarcely any longer expect life to be fair, because we are giving up the assumption that we are entitled to find a moral order in the world laid on for us, prior to our own efforts to set one up. At one time people believed that our various moral institutions, political, legal and religious, were modelled upon and merely topped-up an antecedently-operating cosmic moral Providence. But the duplication involved here was paradoxical. If a supremely wise and effective moral Providence were already in place and working, why the need for such a great battery of imperfect human institutions to supplement it? Couldn't God manage on his own? It seems clear from this that the religious doctrine of a moral Providence at work in the world was to be understood not realistically but regulatively: it was a guiding picture of what a well-run order of things should look like. So here we are already well on the way to acknowledging what is obviously the case, namely that through religion it is we who must make life make sense, we who must tell all the stories, and we who must work out institutional arrangements that will make life a bit less amoral and unjust. The work of God is a work that we have got to do, not a work that has already been done for us. And indeed, if the metaphysical situation is as we have been describing, where else could human values have come from except from human beings, and where else could human linguistic meanings have come from except from human beings? Any other view is absurd. So we are in the Void and we make the lot. Religion exists to give us the strength to do it. And the problem of evil must be seen as a problem that we are to ourselves. Complaining to someone else about it is an abdication. We should refuse the idea of a managing God-out-there who may be summoned to explain the way he administers the world. Instead we should invoke the ideal or regulative God of religion to give us the strength to combat evil. We are the problem and we must ourselves be the solution. The work is ours, and religion is there to help us to do it. Traditionally realistic religion functioned to make people weak, but there is the alternative of a non-realistic kind of religion that functions to make people strong. The old realistically-defined problem of evil was an intellectual and moral self-deception. People know that now, which is why they are refusing the problem as it was traditionally posed.

An interesting sign of the way things are going is the rise of chaos science, which is based on the insight that a physical system whose behaviour is governed by more than three equations may be in principle unpredictable, even at the macro-level. Totalizing doctrines and dreams of omniscience are fading from science as they are from philosophy. We are giving up the idea of tramlines-out-there, and accepting contingency. We are even becoming *untroubled* by the only-human, historically-evolved, improvised and ever-changing character of our moralities, our knowledge-systems and our language.

Fourthly, then, language itself is by far the most wideranging and powerful illustration of our general thesis. Today it has come to seem obvious that language is only human. Such terms as 'language-game' and 'speech-act' serve to remind us of how completely language is tied into doing our human things and transacting the business of human life. Language is everywhere pervaded by human feelings, human valuations, human gender-constructions and human purposes, so that nothing but a human being can be a true speaker. We should not be confused by the outpourings of recordings and synthesizers, which are not true speech. Talking to them is not genuine conversation. To be truly a speaker is by that very fact to be playing a part in human social life, to be transacting human business – in short, speaking is just being human, to such an extent that it is quite unclear to us what a non-human speaker could possibly be.

So if the various lines of thought just summarized converge to show how completely post-metaphysical and post-theistic we are becoming, then language shows it most clearly of all. For twentieth-century thought about language has made God – the old realistically-understood God – terminally silent.

Far back in our past, God was not only the ground of the world-order and the moral order, he was even more, and indeed he was first of all, a language-user. *The* language-user, the First Speaker, Voice (i.e. *vox*, meaning) itself, the one who had called all things into existence.

It has been said recently that we need a better explanation of belief in God than has yet been given, and that the time has perhaps come to write an honest biography of him.[15] Yes, indeed. If we were to try to write such a biography, it would concentrate on God's expression in language and would be divided into three main chapters, entitled Divine Speech, Divine Writing and Divine Silence.[16]

The age of divine speech would cover the preliterate era, during which the human world was ordered and the human self was constituted by the spoken word alone. The most typical religious phenomena of this epoch involved spirits possessing and speaking through the human subject in a state of trance: shamanism, oracles, mediumship and prophecy. Social control beyond earshot depended upon people's hearing authoritative supernatural voices in their heads. There was no other way in which civilization could begin. At first everyone heard the voices, but later they became restricted to certain special places, or induced mental states, or classes of professional ecstatics. Slowly, they faded. But in retrospect people looked back to the archaic period of control by supernatural voices as a Golden Age when there was no moral perplexity, because in those days folk just heard and obeyed. The crucial point to grasp is that human mentality first evolved for the sake of social control. Why else should it ever have developed?

The age of divine writing is the age of scriptural religion, lasting from around 500 BCE until quite recently. It had what now seem to have been a number of very odd features. Scriptural religion was an attempt to conceal, to make up for, and to postpone the consequences of the falling-silent of the old Voice. So the first essential feature of scriptural religion is that it was obliged to blur the distinction between speech and writing. The Word-of-God-here-written claimed to be just as good as the now-silent World-of-God-spoken had formerly been. At every point the scriptural text is trying to persuade the reader – and itself – that it is a kind of gramophone record that successfully preserves the authentic Voice. The Voice is not altogether silent after all, for here it is preserved in a written form that is endlessly replayable, yet always fresh, immediate and to the point. It can guide us today just as reliably as the Voice ringing in their heads guided our forebears. But now we come to the cycle of other doctrines necessary to scriptural religion. In particular, there is a pre-established harmony between the structure of language and the structure of reality, and language can be (the divine language of scripture actually *is*) unchanging and unchangingly matched to the unchanging objective natures of things that it reports, so that there can be an unchanging, omniscient and infallibly veracious language-user whose Word is forever Truth, and whose purposes are unchangingly expressed in the unchanging World that he has spoken and which is now here written down – this text being, in effect, his very own Voice.

So scripture rests on a whole series of beliefs about language. First, that in pre-literate times there really was an immediate guiding presence of an infallible divine Voice. Secondly, that scripture is like an endlessly replayable cassette tape of that Voice, recorded in its later years, always the same, but always relevant and adequate as an infallible guide. And thirdly that language, the language of God can be unchanging and unchangingly completely adequate to lead us through what is, after all, a finite and unchanging set of possible human situations-before-God. Why? – because writing can be unchangeably the master of reality. The claim is that our type of mind, the mind formed by writing, can be as efficiently controlled by scripture as the earlier type of mind, the mind made to hear voices, was controlled by hearing the Voice of God.

If all these notions are true, then there can be a stable literate sacred civilization whose guardian class are the scribes and the exegetes, the Masters of Sacred Letters. But when all these ideas about language collapse utterly, as they progressively did during the nineteenth century, then God falls instantly and utterly silent as we realize that the whole Scriptural epoch was a diversion or postponement – now in brackets, now *over*.

So the third epoch in the life of God begins, the age of Divine Absence. Silence and darkness, forever. A few people who have not yet heard about language fancy that somewhere in their souls they are intuiting non-linguistically a feeling of warmth, as of a Love deep down things. But we have no non-linguistically-shaped experience, and if you are no longer actually hearing from God – that is, if no true *language* is getting through to you – then he is not being experienced at all. And if there cannot be an extra-human language-user, if there is no way in which we who are the only language-users might so use language as to transcend the human realm entirely, if, that is, there is no sense in the idea that language, which is just a lot of human habits, just a humanly-maintained field of differential noises and marks,[17] could possibly be so used as to transcend the human realm which it constitutes, then the world of language has no outside. Nothing wholly extra-human can get through to us in it, and we cannot use it to transcend itself so as to make contact with something extra-human.

Some theologians seek to escape this conclusion by maintaining that the God of the Bible, being the Lord of history, has revealed himself not in words but in a chain of historical events, and in particular in the human person of Jesus of Nazareth. But the question of language cannot be thus bypassed, for there are of course no historical events without a description in language of what they are and what they are taken to mean, and there is no Jesus of Nazareth until he is named and described in language. So a dilemma still returns: all those descriptive sentences in the Bible which identify the saving acts of God and his work in Christ have got to be human sentences, couched in a changing human vocabulary and subject to endless paraphrases, reinterpretations and the like. In no way can they *both* be human-in-a-human-language *and* also emanate from an extra-human speaker who uses them in such a way as to express a supra-historical, fixed and unchanging truth. So we still cannot conceive how there could be an old-style divine Revelation in the human world, now seen to be a world of language.

A Bible, a work of scripture, is an anthology of precious recollections of a Voice, gathered in great haste before it fell silent. It is a text that cannot help but try to suggest to us that when we read it we are not just reading, but hearing. Jeremiah's text is a particularly touching and quaint illustration of the paradoxes. More than almost any other writer in the Hebrew Bible Jeremiah gives a vivid impression of emergent subjectivity, but just because he is becoming so subjective he is finding the Voice more difficult to hear. He is on the hinge between speech and writing. He is himself turning into a writer, for he dictates to a scribe and distributes his own writings to be read by others. Subjective, a writing man who is already as much poet as prophet, Jeremiah was presumably the first in Israel to be reduced to hearing God by the indirect route of eating written words. He certainly makes the connection between writing and subjectivity clear enough:

> Thy words were found, and I ate them,
>> and thy words became to me a joy
>> and the delight of my heart;
> for I am called by thy name,
>> O Lord, God of Hosts.
> I did not sit in the company of merrymakers,
>> nor did I rejoice;
> I sat alone because thy hand was upon me . . .

> (Jeremiah 15.16f.; and for Jeremiah on writing, see also 17.1; 22.30; 25.13, 29–32, 36, 45; 51.60ff.)

After Jeremiah, the word of God is increasingly received in written form (e.g. Ezekiel 2.9–3.3). Ecstatics gradually turn into writers and prophets into apocalyptists. Even God employs a secretary, the recording angel. By the time it ends, the Bible seems ready to admit that it really *is* writing. It ends with the Epistles and with the Apocalypse, works which make no attempt to conceal their own literariness.

So the Bible could be read – though it has never yet been read – as educating us to accept that the Voice is silent, and we must henceforth be content with writing. At first the Bible itself cannot accept this. When it opens, in Genesis, there is a gulf between medium and message. This is a text, yet it tells of how *spoken* Words of command created the universe and how God walked in the Garden of Eden and *talked* with our first parents. Here is writing, which is only secondary, pretending to put us in touch with an original and primary immediacy. But by the end of the Bible such pretensions have been renounced. We are ready to learn in human writing that religion really is just human writing. Medium and message fall into step with each other.

Do we understand what this signifies? The Bible itself testifies that God is falling silent, and that the original pure immediacy of Voice was mythical. The Bible itself prefigures the age of divine absence into which we have now entered. The whole twenty-four-century 'historical' epoch ruled by the myth of Divine Writing (unchangingly authoritative writing, accurately transcribing pure immediacy, whose meaning was divinely and therefore permanently fixed), was only transitional and disciplinary. It always foreshadowed its own self-dissolution. The biblical books do after all bear the names of human authors. In a sense they all know, they obviously know, that they themselves are only occasional, only human, and only writings. It was a yearning illusory nostalgia for the Voice that spread over all this diverse material the ideology of 'the inspired Word of God' – a phrase which implies a claim that this text is more than just writing, for it is writing breathed-into and charged-up with the supernatural energy of divine speech. Evidently, we couldn't bear the thought that religion is something human, changing, written and therefore open to various interpretations. So we called it all 'the Word of God' and 'Divine Revelation'. But we undid ourselves by making a *revealing* error. We attributed to the Word of God both pure immediacy and unchangeableness. We thought of it in an oddly blurred way that tried to efface the distinction between speech and writing, so that God's Holy Word could have both the permanent long-distance public availability of writing and also the unmistakable immediacy and authority traditionally imputed to divine speech. The contradiction of trying to pretend that writing can somehow, while remaining truly writing, yet be also something more than mere writing, comes out hilariously in Jeremiah himself. For the prophet tells us, in *writing* of a *letter* he wrote, in which God *says* that since Israel didn't obey the old *written* law he will give them a new law, *written*(!) in their hearts, which they will unfailingly obey. Why? Because there is a great difference in status between *writing* on tablets of stone and *writing* on tablets of flesh, and the

New Testament duly makes much of it. But what on earth can it be? Writing is still writing whatever it is written on, be it stone or flesh. And while we are on the point, let us not fail to notice that for centuries the fundamental Christian claim vis-à-vis Judaism was that whereas the Jewish religion is based on a written law, the New Testament is – what? Something more than writing? So there is what now looks like a very strange double sophistry at the heart of early Christian apologetics. It seemed to be trying to claim in writing that the gospel is more than writing – even though in fact it no longer contains the 'Thus saith the Lord' of the old prophets. It is evidently less immediate, yet seems to claim to be more so.

In conclusion, God was originally a supposed pure immediacy of Voice, by which the human self was once constituted and human life was guided. In the so-called Axial Age, 25–30 centuries ago, the Voice was falling silent. Scriptural religion arose to try to preserve it. The age of scriptural religion is an age of strict social discipline, the clerkly ruling group maintaining tight control of meaning and a very clear confusion between writing and speech. The people must be made to believe that the Book is as good as the Voice, and as such is an unambiguously authoritative guide to faith and conduct. Yet the Book itself internally undermines these very ideas. In any case, between the seventeenth and nineteenth centuries they broke down for good. Now the Voice really *has* ceased, and a crisis successfully deferred for millennia has at last broken.[18]

9. Into the Void

Scriptural religion – so we have argued – was a long and remarkably effective postponement. By various devices it sustained the paradoxical belief that human writings could maintain amongst us the long-lost immediacy of the divine Voice. When the paradox was exposed and the devices broke down, it was as if people suddenly realized that God had not actually been heard from in person for ages. Consider the present-day situation in Catholicism:

divine figures no longer speak, nor even appear. All that is left is appearances of Mary, which take place in relatively backward regions of the world. Although she is still seen, Mary hardly ever speaks. And people accept this, as if they recognize that nothing more vivid than that is to be expected nowadays.

In the early Enlightenment the response of the leading intellectual figures to this fading of the gods was generally optimistic. It was felt that 'man had come of age'. They were optimistic because they believed that reality was still in place, and that consciousness, Truth and Value were still in place. Only in the later nineteenth century did it finally become clear that this was not so. If we are always stuck inside language, culture, interpretation and historical change, then we are stuck inside our own merely-contingent and shifting thought-patterns, without any 'hard' and independent touchstones of reality, meaning, truth and value. Now everything begins to dissolve. For many centuries – in fact, since the rise of philosophy – it has been of the greatest importance to us that we should be able to distinguish between appearance and reality, between the way things seem to us and the way they really are, between interpretation and fact, between wishes, dreams and fancies and what is objectively the case. And we are ceasing to be sure that we have any touchstone or criterion for making these distinctions. Plato is dead. Fact and fiction are becoming inextricable. We are returning to primitive thought. The best measure of how far we have already gone is the extent to which philosophy and theology have vanished from people's view as serious subjects. They were all about how to distinguish the Truth from idolatory, heresy and superstition, reality from appearance, and they have largely faded – as indeed the 'academic' ideal itself has also faded. Postmodernity is a flux of images and fictions. The dominant intellectuals are imaginative writers, novelists, dramatists, film directors, entertainers. Philosophy (in the persons of, for example, Nietzsche, the later Heidegger, and now, very clearly, late Rorty) has argued itself out of its own historic claims and into legitimating those whom Plato calls compendiously 'the poets'. We have lost the ability to make and hold on to the great distinctions by which, historically, capital-P Philosophy put down fancy, exalted Reason, and set the intellectual world in place. One may be cheerful or pessimistic about the resulting cultural situation, but at any rate it is a rather novel one. Its sources go back to the beginnings of the Romantic movement, but it has become fully developed only with the arrival of the consumerist or media society in the second half of the twentieth century. And, as we have suggested, its crucial feature is the disappearance of the real, our growing incapacity – our lack, even, of the *will* – to separate truth from fiction, the objectively real from the flux of human interpretations.

In my house there is a wall to which a row of coatpegs are fixed. Over the years these hooks have entirely vanished beneath layer upon layer of coats, hats, scarves, sticks, leads, satchels and other objects. The coatpegs beneath are no longer visible; in fact, they haven't been seen at all for years. It is no longer easy even to guess just where they are, so large is the mound of clothing heaped over them.

Thus it is with the way our language and our cultural interpretations have covered over the world. Realists claim that there must still be a row of pegs underneath there to support all the hats and coats. But since we are always already in language and culture, that is, the world is always already covered over with our interpretative concepts, the pegs never get seen. They are always already hidden by coats. It is hard to see why the realist clings so tenaciously to a claim that never gets verified.

What are the pegs? The empiricist-Kantian view says that the pegs are the raw data of sense-experience, and the hats and coats are the general concepts that we impose upon those data by way of organizing them to make a rationalized, intelligible world. Kant's account is too familiar, so instead let us quote William James' summary list of the basic commonsense concepts that we impose upon our experience, as given in Lecture V of *Pragmatism* (1907).[19] They are:

> Thing
> The same or different

Kinds
Minds
Bodies
One Time
One Space
Subjects and attributes
Causal influences
The fancied
The real

At first sight this looks a little like Kant's list of Categories of the
Understanding. Not so. For James, these general notions were
'discovered' and found to work by our remote ancestors. But they
are used in many ways and in very varying degrees. Unlike Kant,
for whom strictly rule-governed application of the concepts was
a necessary condition for there being any objective knowledge of
the world, James the psychologist emphasizes how partial and
how casual is our use of them: 'It is only the smallest part of his
experience's flux that anyone actually does straighten out by
applying to it these conceptual instruments.'[20] James is critical of
the rationalist philosophy that attempts 'to eternalize the commonsense categories by treating them very technically and articu-
lately'. Such eternalizing flies in the face of the evidence of human
variability, cultural difference, historical change, and the developed natural sciences (which considerably modify commonsense
and therefore relativize its categories). A good, though post-
Jamesian, illustration is the way in which the one, mathematized
linear Time of Newton and Kant only became an established
world-wide social fact with the arrival of Greenwich Mean Time
and near-simultaneous worldwide communications – by which
time developments in physics had already reduced it to merely
pragmatic status anyway. So the effect of James' discussion is to
emphasize how multi-levelled, how variable, how pragmatic and
often how very informal are people's constructions of their
worlds.

On William James' account, then, the way all the clobber hangs on the pegs is pretty casual and disorderly. In any case, 'the pegs' are only the flux of sense-experience. It's *given*, but that is about all there is to say for it, for in itself it is neither real nor unreal, neither true nor false, and (one might well conclude) neither here nor there.

An alternative way of answering the question of what the pegs are is to say that the pegs are to the coats as particular things with proper names are to the various descriptions that we hang upon them. The pegs are the referents of discourse. They are the points at which language is hooked-on to objects. 'Existents' literally 'stand out' like pegs. In principle, each could be made the bearer of a proper name. Admittedly, it may be said, the ways in which we describe the world in language are as variable and untidy as the ways in which my children threw their innumerable coats over the pegs. But under the heap we may perhaps still be able to discern the zigzag line of the pegs. Beneath the surface confusion, a formal pattern can just be made out. So why should not a 'critical realist' similarly claim that beneath the jumble of our piled-up linguistic clothing of the world there is a pattern of mathematical relationships between particular things, a pattern that science can abstract and define?

This sort of critical realism fails, because the mathematical pattern is not itself the pegs. It is only another coat, something *we* impose upon the world, a tool that *we* may use in devising predictions and so forth. Maybe it works, maybe it works very well, maybe it works every time. But it is only a formal pattern. Its admitted applicability or utility falls far short of the objective 'reality' that critical realism looks for. There still have to be pegs for the pattern to be attached to, and not only are such pegs not given, one doesn't even see how they could be given. Reference itself is just another linguistic operation, and there is no reason to attribute to it a magic capacity to jump out of language that other linguistic operations lack.

So, I am saying that our linguistic and our mathematical descriptions and interpretations cover the world over completely, making the thing-in-itself as inaccessible as God. Just attend to whatever is nearest to hand at this moment. Attend now to your own attention to it, and you'll see that you can only get hold of a thing by so-to-say absorbing it into the stream of language that is you. In old-fashioned terms, you get hold of the object by throwing general concepts over it like big rings over a vertical post, until the post becomes definable as the point at which all the rings overlap with each other. In slightly less old-fashioned terms, we apprehend the empirical object as a tangle of words, interpretations, signs. As people gingerly pick up a spider with a duster, so we apprehend objects by wrapping them up in language.

In postmodern or anti-foundationalist thinking the world thus seems to become like literature, all metaphors, interpretations, deceptions – *writing*. There isn't any longer any Archimedean point from which the world can be understood as it really is. Indeed, the notion of what is really, objectively, factually and literally just true (whatever anyone thinks, so *there!*) – that notion has ceased to be useful.

Freud's work illustrates the point here particularly well. He has too often been criticized from the point of view of orthodox scientific and philosophical empiricism, by people who have failed to see how original he was in breaking with the assumptions of Cartesian-empiricist thought. The main epistemological tradition had always been committed to separating out and rejecting the false. But Freud did not need to do this. He was able to make good use of our lies, our deceptions, our fantasies, our errors and our hypocrisies.[21] He did not need to prioritize straight and truthful *oratio recta*, direct speech, in quite the old way. Whatever you produced was grist to his mill, and in this respect he was a true postmodern, able to accept and to use fictions, fantasies and untruths as part of what we are. They too were interpretations, to be further interpreted and commented on. From this seemingly beginningless, endless and even rather arbitrary process of interpretation and reinterpretation emerged understanding and healing.

Normally, our ideas about the growth of understanding imply something like an approximationist philosophy of science. One who gains in understanding has thereby got a bit closer to the real Truth. Maybe that real Truth is no more than an ideal standard which can only be approached and will never actually be reached by human beings, but 'critical realists' still require the real Truth as a regulative Ideal or a reference point. The argument is essentially that of St Thomas Aquinas's Fourth Way of proving God: for talk about different degrees of understanding to be meaningful there must be a yardstick, namely, a complete understanding of the whole Truth. How can there be fractions except in relation to a Whole?

Freud, however, does not require the notion of a final understanding of the whole Truth. There isn't a whole Truth about a human being, and there isn't anything for *complete* self-knowledge to be. There is no sure progress in self-understanding. Freud has to be content with secondariness forever. In Nietzsche's dramatic imagery, we are mask behind mask, indefinitely. No real core-self is reached. We are continually reinventing ourselves, immersed in a world of fictions and reinterpretations.

III

THE TURNING

1. A philosophical revelation

Our thinking and behaviour are constrained in deep and non-obvious ways by society and by our ancestors. Perhaps this accounts for the most pervasive and puzzling feature of human thought to date, namely the fact that until very recently people everywhere believed that life's wires are pulled by hidden entities. The manifest world, the world of appearance, is subordinated to a higher-ranking invisible world-beyond on which it is founded, by which it is explained, controlled and given value, and for the sake of which it exists. Typical invisible entities that are still widely postulated even today include minds, acts of will, scientific laws and the meanings of words. Others include the many objects postulated by philosophers and theologians, where these are thought of as being 'more real' than what is readily apparent or manifest in the world of ordinary life and ordinary language. From Plato to Kant at least, philosophers sought knowledge of a kind of invisible architecture behind or beyond the world of appearance. They tried to purify and discipline their minds so that they could handle abstractions in a vocabulary rigorously controlled, completely general and very powerful. Their hope was that a super-science of the hidden controlling principles would explain the world and show us how to live. The aims of theology were much the same. It sought to put us in touched with the unseen Powers that be, so that enjoying their favour, and guided by

83

them along the right path of life, we might at last achieve eternal happiness.

All these ways of thinking are so deeply engrained in our vocabulary, and therefore in us, that the thought that they are at an end still produces the effect we have called nihilism. 'So there is no Truth, nothing's real, nothing makes sense, nothing's worth while.' People say all this just because all their ideas of Truth, reality, sense and value remain profoundly platonic to this day. To lose platonic realism seems to be to lose everything. We are so accustomed to the devaluation of the here-and-now in favour of something better behind it that when the invisible fades the here-and-now does not recover its value. It stays devalued. Hence nihilism. Nor does the story end there, for people then start nostalgically looking for ways of conquering nihilism by reinstating the invisible world. They hope to conquer nihilism by going back to the very ways of thinking that produced it in the first place.

A religious example: a good and kind friend, commiserating with me about what he saw as my theological troubles, said: 'Well, you're still a seeker, like the rest of us.' I had to upset him by saying that I am not a seeker. Plato left us with the idea that Truth is out there and all-important – but some way off. It needs to be pursued, and the virtues that will be most helpful are rigorous honesty and whole-heartedness. Good people are therefore people whose lives are dedicated to seeking a great blessedness-giving Meaning or Truth of things that lies just over the horizon. Life is a question that has an Answer, and we ought to be out there looking for it. A religious person, a believer, is a person who has found her Answer and now adheres tenaciously to her personally-discovered set of blessedness-giving, life's-problem-solving tenets. It is a very good thing indeed to be a believer in this sense, so if you haven't yet got your set of tenets-about-the-hidden but are nevertheless evidently a decent person, why then, you must obviously be a seeker, because all the good people either have a creed or are looking for one. Everybody needs a creed. There's no lasting happiness without one. And so on ... but I had to say to my friend that it seems to me that all the assumptions behind that word 'seeker' have broken down. How do we *know* that life's a riddle to which there is a great unifying Answer ready and waiting for us just around the corner? How do we *know* that we should spend our lives searching for it because, when we find it, it will bring us eternal happiness? I have been suggesting that the entire way of thinking which vested supreme truth and value in an unseen controlling realm-beyond is at an end. I am also suggesting that honesty, self-control and wholeheartedness of the kind that platonism recommended may not be so desirable either. For it often seems nowadays that the masked obliquity of actors and dramatists and the reckless blasphemies of great imaginative writers are by far superior to the straightforward decency of the honest and singleminded. Lies and deceptions can be truer than Truth. Furthermore, earlier in this very paragraph my use of the phrases 'her set' and 'your set of tenets' betrayed the breakdown of platonism, for it showed that the most we can in practice think of people as attaining and being satisfied with is a personal truth, that is, a man-made truth and not the old sort of objective Truth. There are regional truths, but nobody today is going to specify just what is the One True Truth, assert that it is objective and compulsory for everyone everywhere, and defend it as sovereign with equal assurance in all companies, whether liberal, Muslim, marxist, Catholic, or Jewish. The derogatory use of the term 'fundamentalism' shows that old-style claims to exclusive possession of the One True Truth are not now to be taken seriously.

All this means that we are undergoing a major intellectual conversion or Turning. We are ceasing to believe that truth is ever something given from Beyond to the purified soul, and we are instead coming to think of truth as something plural, something generated by the play of language, something that we ourselves create and continually recreate. And we are ceasing to believe in any world-beyond at all. Today's philosophers are busily hunting down and destroying the last remnants of that idea.

The Turning requires us to start thinking about religion and philosophy in quite new ways. So far as philosophy is concerned, we already have several eloquent and effective statements. Wittgenstein's *Investigations* I, §§98–133 is especially clear. Philosophy is not a superscience. It does not purport to give us extra information about the hidden. It merely assembles reminders and helps us to see the obvious. 'Since everything lies open to view there is nothing to explain.' Philosophy is an activity. It works continually to do itself out of a job, by curing the cramps and discomforts that first led people to turn to it.

Very clear. And it might be supposed that a parallel transformation of religious thinking would be quite easy to carry through. We have only to give up the idea that religious doctrines supply extra information about hidden beings and hidden machinery. Instead we should see religious doctrines as helping to facilitate the 360-degree turn by which we spin right round and come back to see ordinary reality afresh. On this account the new philosophy of religion will be equivalent to what theologians call 'realized eschatology'. The basic recommendation is, 'Don't project it up into a world above, and don't defer it all to a future world yet to come. Instead, see it all as being realized now.' On this view (for which there is a great deal of New Testament evidence) we should regard our fellow human beings as people who are already children of God, already forgiven, already risen, ascended and glorified. The maxim is that it's all true already. So preaching the gospel is not a way of supplying people with novel information but rather a way of opening their eyes to what is already the case about themselves. Conversion is a freshening of our vision, and not a vision of wholly fresh objects. Realized eschatology equals, therefore, a regulative or non-cognitive philosophy of religion. Doctrine *is* ethics. That is, doctrines shape attitudes and behaviour, which in turn create reality – and so the doctrines preached and lived create their own truth. Orthopraxis is the watchword. Religion is not a vision of another world, but a re-vision of this world.

That is fine, so far as it goes. The main trouble is that it only works successfully so long as the people don't understand it. It works fine among unphilosophical people, while we remain at the fuzzy, confused level at which preaching (and most theology) operates. But when people are led to see the language a little more clearly they will of course describe it as atheism and reject it out of hand. In a way they are right to be so suspicious, for we ourselves also find that there are acute difficulties in stating the religious meaning of the new situation clearly.

Let me try to make the unclarity clear. One fine day in March 1984 I stood on the pavement in Shepherd's Bush, West London, talking with a friend during a break from work. As some people walked by I heard them exchange a few words in a foreign language. The words were opaque to me, because I lacked the social training in their culture that would have enabled me to make appropriate sounds back and so begin to interact successfully with those people. In a flash, then, I jumped from the opacity of that particular snatch of conversation to the opacity of language in general. It is only human, just a lot of contingent noises and marks by which we are trained to adapt our behaviour to each other. We human beings speak only to each other, and only among ourselves. This communicative life of ours is foundationless and outsideless. How could language possibly take us right outside our human world and our human point of view? There is no outside. We always find ourselves already inside a language that was in place before we came along. We don't make it, it makes us. We are inside it, not it inside us. Even the inwardness or subjectivity that we feel we have, and which Tennyson and Wordsworth have described so well, is only a literary effect produced by our acquired skill in using the indexical pronouns. You were simply taught to speak of yourself as an I that can regard itself as a me, and is accountable. Our social and linguistic training goes all the way down, and there is no bedrock human essence prior to it. Otherwise put, my mother tongue goes straight through my head from ear to ear. It shapes me completely. I cannot step out of this present flow of language-moulded thought and experience. Every attempt to step out of it only brings me promptly back into it. Efforts to escape are as misguided as trying to go on walking in a northerly direction after you have reached the North Pole. And the proof that we are caught within the end-less flowing metaphoricity of language lies in the realization that any talk of 'stepping out' or 'escaping' from the metaphorical merely adds to it. These are metaphors, too. But now I realized that an outsideless prison is not a prison.[1] *There is only this!* This contingent flow of verbal signifiers in which I am caught up, and which is outsideless, must be Being-itself, absolute Reality.

I felt dizzy, a full second having now passed, and gripped a railing. Psychologically it was as if I was getting a supernatural revelation. But this was an anti-revelation. I was not getting any additional information from outside the human realm. The mess-age was that there is no message. I was bowled over by the thought of outsidelessness. It had suddenly removed our inherited way of characterizing the here and now as being merely finite, contingent, relative, temporal and so on. All those terms, which come from platonism, are polar. The here-and-now has been defined by con-trasting it with something bigger and better beyond it, some-thing necessary, enduring and timeless. But when I saw the utter outsidelessness of the here-and-now it had lost the contrast through which it had always hitherto been constituted as itself. Hence my giddiness and disorientation. It was a revelation of the utter gratuitousness, but therefore also the sublimity, of empirical existence. Outsideless and not needing to rest upon anything other than itself, the here-and-now suddenly became like God. The moment, fleeting and infinitely insignificant, was revealed as all there is, self-subsistent, Being-itself. René Descartes had come to this point, for when he had established the *Cogito*, 'I think there-fore I am', *a priori* and at first outsidelessly, he was briefly forced to wonder if perchance he were himself God.[2] He hastily retreated, and restored the old platonic contrasts. No, I am not God, he said, for I am conscious of my own imperfection, and I have an idea of a perfection that I am not. So Descartes very wisely bolted for safety. But we can't. For us, the living movement of the sign in the here and now really *is* outsideless, making me incurably giddy because I don't know how to express the religious meaning of our new situation except by going back to, and misusing, precisely the old obsolete platonic contrasts. I start saying that we must learn to see in the here and now, in the only human, in the unstable and fleeting sign . . . what? The absolute in the relative, the infinite in the finite, the eternal in the fleeting. Thus I both talk nonsense and perpetuate the very vocabulary I said we ought to be trying to get away from. But what other terminology do we have? Clutching the railing and still trying to get around the thought of outsidelessness, I thought, 'Transient as all this is, there isn't and there cannot be anything for us but this, so this transient is the Necessary.' Back into Plato again.

This discussion is suggesting a very curious conclusion, namely that religious thought is even more deeply in hock to platonism than is philosophy itself, and finds it much harder to escape. Suppose I say that religion is to see Eternity in a grain of sand, or the divine Christ in a needy fellow human, or whatever: in every such case I draw upon the old platonic contrasts of eternal/temporal, universal/particular, infinite/finite and so forth. I may negate them, I may bend them, I may metaphoricize them, I may twist them rhetorically in a variety of ways. But whatever I do, I can't help but effectively concede the logical priority of the platonic scheme of thought. Platonism still provides the standing intellectual framework within which the games of religious language are played. The development of more symbolist, more regulative and more non-realist accounts of the status of religious language only confirms the continuing priority of the platonic contrasts. And it is just those contrasts that are the problem. If platonism and its ways of thinking are at last fading out of the culture we want to know if there can be religious thought completely independent of the old platonic framework.

Now I am moving into retrospect for a moment, for it has become clear to me why I had my philosophical revelation in Shepherd's Bush. When someone is badly blocked, when the available vocabulary just cannot be made to say what one urgently feels, then a quasi-religious experience is the usual result. Language had gone opaque, I felt lost and disoriented, and there was a feeling of an Ineffable on the point of expression but somehow not quite able to achieve it. For years I had been getting more and more naturalistic in outlook, more concerned about language, and more preoccupied with the struggle to slough off platonism. The paragraphs above about my philosophical revelation are steeped in literary references. They show the influences that converged to produce a few seconds of giddiness and a burst of frustrated sentences.

The sentences ran something like this: 'The here and now of language, purely human and purely contingent though it be, has to be religiously ultimate and Good enough for us. This the manifest, elusive and fleeting, is all there can be, all there is, all there need be for us. It is sufficient. This human word is as it were the Word of God. The desire to escape from it is a symptom of confusion, sickness or treachery. Since this–now is outsidelessly all-there-is, I must regard it as the very presencing of Being-itself. Heidegger. But, dammit, even as I say these words to myself, I've still got Plato on my back!'

Spinoza was a bit like this, trying to articulate thoroughgoing religious naturalism in a scholastic vocabulary. Meanwhile, I was talking to my friend. As you may guess, it was no kind of deep or intense conversation, because the talk of English men is in the very highest degree mild, devious, allusive, ironical and indirect. Self-deprecating, inconsequential, fine-spun – I needn't go on: it is the strangest paradox of English culture that while we remain (or seem to remain) intellectually in bondage to Plato and Aristotle, our manner of speech among ourselves has for a century and a half been postmodern. Very odd. Anyway, it was the ordinary English kind of desultory small-talk, thickly-sown with mines and wispy with loose ends, that was the background to my revelation.

The end of metaphysics, the death of God, nihilism and postmodernism are just some of the words used to describe the cultural condition of a people for whom Plato's intellectual and religious legacy is now quite spent, exhausted and dissolved, but who have as yet no satisfactory vocabulary for the new situation. Roughly, we want a vocabulary that is not binary, not hierarchizing, and that does not devalue the manifest in favour of something beyond that is bigger, better and invisible. But where is this new language we need?

2. Poiesis

Religious supernaturalism commonly pictures religious truth as being given to us from Above, as if it were timeless news about timeless objects. But in a religion of redemption, and (above all) in a secular and historically-minded age, faith must come down to earth. Religion must be seen instead as a way of creatively reimagining or refashioning the world of everyday life.

Nor is this idea entirely new. We have already mentioned the most instructive precedent, the one that theologians call 'realized eschatology'. This is a line of thought already prominent in the New Testament, whereby events, powers and themes that belong to the Last Days and the future blessed world are seized in advance and brought forward into this present world. The rationale for this is, in a broad sense, philosophical. The old Hebraic idea of human history as a salvation-drama controlled by God appears to picture God as an historical agent, who through a long series of actions in time progressively modifies his own relationship to us and our standing before him. But this sounds too anthropomorphic. If God is really powerful and really in charge, he must surely be eternally the same and have eternally preplanned the whole drama. In which case the religious perfecting of reality should be seen not so much as an unfolding sequence of supernaturally-caused events, but rather as an eternal truth to which people's eyes need only be opened. We ought to live as if everyone and everything had already died and risen with Christ. One should see everything as being already ransomed, healed, restored, forgiven. The believer *actively imputes redemption* to the world, living in such a way as to help make the deep truth of the world's already-redeemedness manifest.

The sources of this theology are plain enough. They include the Lutheran idea of a righteousness first divinely imputed and then progressively actualized in the believer's life, the Kantian idea of religious doctrines as regulative or action-guiding, and the nineteenth-century idea of the Christian life as a work of making-manifest the reign of God on Earth. Above all there is the theology of F. D. Maurice, whose thought united realized eschatology with platonism and Christian socialism. Timeless truths are to be made into social facts.

During the Indian summer of biblical theology in the 1950s these ideas were almost standard doctrine. They could be so expressed as to sound very like non-realism. There is not very much difference between so acting as to make a hidden truth manifest, and so acting as to make a dream or vision come true. We earlier quoted John Robinson crossing the line, when he says of evils like cancer that 'God is to be found in them rather than by turning away from them. Love is there to be met, responded to, *and created* through them and out of them.'[3] By writing 'Love', not 'God', at the head of his second sentence Robinson veils his own indiscretion, and then by italicizing *'and created'* he flaunts it again – a typically teasing double-take. In any case, Robinson's refusal of the problem of evil is by implication non-realistic. God is not to be thought of as a Being out there who controls all events so as to make them fulfil a moral purpose.

However, I have already suggested that a non-realist interpretation of mainline religion will not serve as an answer to today's needs, because it must still call upon a platonic vocabulary to explain itself. It needs all the classic distinctions between the ideal and the actual, reality and appearance, rules and instances, the un-changing and the changing and so forth. But today platonism, and these distinctions, are under fierce attack.

All this must be spelled out. The old Cambridge Biblical Theology of C. H. Dodd, C. F. D. Moule, J. A. T. Robinson and others was much vexed about the question of the Wrath of God and Christ's propitiation of God. To get over the moral difficulty of such ideas they read the New Testament in markedly platonic terms. God's disposition towards us is timeless. It is only we who differ in our various personal responses to God's Love, and only we who change. So, speaking about the Wrath of God in his lectures on *Romans* in the 1950s, Robinson said: 'The same sun that melts the wax hardens the clay.' When, twenty years later, those old lectures were published, Robinson clearly recognized that to speak of the Wrath of God as an automatic mechanism, operating perhaps like cirrhosis of the liver, and with nothing personal about it, was simply incompatible with the rest of his own teaching. So he attempted to personalize God's Wrath a little. To experience it really is to experience *God*. However:

> It is not he who has gone sour on us, but we on him: being what we are, we are capable of knowing the wine of his love only as the vinegar of his wrath. *He* has not changed – the revelation of his righteousness and of his wrath are in fact one and the same revelation . . .[4]

But in this later text the metaphor, of wine experienced as tasting sour like vinegar, is still impersonal. The love of God is impartial and unchanging. The Wrath of God is love's effect upon the obdurate human heart that rejects it. God does not personally single us out for damnation; rather, we condemn ourselves by the way we respond or fail to respond to him. Once again it is *we* who do all the work and make all the difference. Although they themselves were rather unphilosophical, the philosophical upshot of what the Cambridge theologians were saying was that the metaphors of religious language do not give information about God, but instead function to guide our action – for example, by symbolizing the long-term effects of our choices.

In a similar vein, these theologians argued that contrary to what seems to be said in Romans 3.25, I John 2.2, 4.10 (AV and RV), Christ does not propitiate an angry God, but rather is sent by God to be the expiation for our sins. So it's not that God changes from being angered to being loving, but that we are changed by being cleansed of our sinfulness. And such was the influence of these theologians (and especially of Dodd, who was their master[5]) that the more recent translations (RSV and NEB) have in all three verses duly replaced the word 'propitiation' by 'expiation' or 'remedy'. The same theologians also loved to quote II Corinthians 5.19: 'God was in Christ reconciling the world to himself', stressing that Paul does not say that God was reconciling himself to the world. God, we are being told, is not the capricious, angry figure of Freudian polemic, nor are Judgment, condemnation and Hell just events and places of the future. Condemnation is *already* the state of those who reject the light, as in the Fourth Gospel (e.g., John 3.16–20). We judge ourselves by the way we respond to the unchanging divine love.

This line of interpretation, derived from F. D. Maurice in particular, lets God off the hook but at a price. It is barely distinguishable from non-realism. God has become a kind of timeless unvarying principle, a radiant standard, and the whole spectrum of differences to be found in the human world is now seen as produced entirely by us.[6] This accords well with the modern Christian humanist stress on our moral responsibility. In relation to both the problem of human sinfulness and the problem of suffering, the divine Love and the divine Grace are seen as constants. What makes the difference is the varied manners in which we humans respond to God's Love and avail ourselves of his Grace. And despite all Robinson's protestations to the contrary, the effect of thus farming all the making-of-a-difference out to us must leave God looking more like a principle or a *façon de parler* than a person. An important controversy of the early nineteenth century has been repeated: God has ceased to be a catastrophist, and has become a uniformitarian. In the nineteenth century ad hoc divine interventions got squeezed out of geology; in the twentieth century we have seen them getting squeezed out of *religion*.

In its heyday the liberal biblical theology certainly passed for orthodox. Yet it had very considerably demythologized ancient and ever-popular ideas of an interventionist God who proves he is personal by actively and personally managing all events. The liberal God was getting to be so non-interventionist and so non-changing that he was becoming non-personal and increasingly non-real. Was he not just a mythical personification of the virtue of agapeistic love?

We see now why the Cambridge liberal theology of the *Soundings* group and others[7] ran into crisis and came to an end. From the best of motives they had sought to demythologize away the more repressive and even sadistic, the more interventionist and even interfering, elements in the idea of God. They came to speak of God as an unchanging Love, completely general and impartial and not detectably or differentially active. As they skirted ever closer to non-realism, the liberals became ever more dependent upon the ancient platonic vocabulary for preserving some measure of objectivity or ontic realism in their talk of God. It was their residual platonism that helped them to hypostatize an unchanging divine Love as a real divine Being, that gave them the appearance-reality distinction that they so much needed, that saw the moral life as a variable human response to an unvarying absolute Standard, and so on. Unluckily for these liberals, though, they were becoming more dependent upon platonism in just the decades when it was finally disappearing. They might disregard Nietzsche, misunderstand Wittgenstein and avoid taking up the challenge of verificationism,[8] but they could not stop the idea of deep historical change from catching up with them eventually. For if there is deep historical change; if, for example, meanings are not laid up in eternity but are socially produced within history, then platonism must pass away. Platonism is needed by those who would claim that there is a divine Love out there that never changes, a Gospel out there that never changes, and some level of human nature that never changes. But if there is history, then everything that is said about the divine Love, the gospel and human nature, is constructed within history, and in different ways in different historical periods. If there is history, then all readings of the New Testament text and of the first-century world are themselves also historically conditioned. The mediaeval New Testament, the Reformation's New Testament, the nineteenth-century New Testament and today's New Testament are different from each other. For centuries people have believed themselves to be getting in touch with the real, original meaning of the New Testament – but of course the supposed 'original meanings' have themselves proved to be historically variable, being constructed very differently in different historical periods. Meaning does not inhere self-identically and timelessly in the graphic signifiers of the New Testament text; rather, those black marks produce different effects and give rise to different commentaries and interpretations as they enter into and mingle with the vocabularies and forms of life of different later periods. So the imputation of a meaning to the New Testament text is and has to be a productive work of the reader's imagination. The book's meaning for us is our fiction. If there is history, we have to break with the old platonic vocabulary and accept the full responsibility (which is ours, anyway) for constantly reinventing our own religious beliefs.

What precisely this involves and what the point of it is, we have still to say. Let us begin by reflecting on the Turning. It is evidently a reversal in religious thought, brought about by the end of platonism. In platonic realism the movement of thought was always from There to here, from the Real out there to the here-and-now as an inferior refraction of it. This way of thinking identified religion with ulteriority, self-disparagement and deference to that out-there which is infinitely greater than oneself. I am mere flesh, temporal, contingent, weak and ignorant by contrast with that which is spirit, eternal, necessary, almighty and all-knowing. But the new concept of religion is going to see it as a fully-immanent productive activity. Religion is a here-and-now conquering of nihilism and a re-creation of our world out of nothing by continually generating new metaphors and new interpretations. We human beings are linguistic animals. We live in a world of signs, and indeed are made of signs. We can live only in communication. So religion is a kind of creative art by which we make ourselves and our world, endlessly revaluing the familiar and minting new metaphors. All major cultures have their own characteristic set of religious metaphors and rituals, and in every culture the central religious concepts and symbols provide the vocabulary in which people articulate their sense of life's meaning and worth. Religion is only human, but no culture survives long without it. Life's meaningfulness and worthwhileness are not given but have to be made, and that making is religion.

What is the new religious object? It is the moving moment in which desire (libido, the life-impulse) comes or is lured into symbolic expression as meaning and is felt as value. This moment is not atomic or substantial, but is a moving difference. The religious concern is for the most intense and deep experience of life – eternal life, abundant life. And since meaning and valuation are social before they are individual, we are not here thinking primarily of religion as working within the inner theatre of individual subjectivity, but of the religion of the public world.

In the older religious thought the creation of the universe was ascribed to God and was called ktisis. For the new way of thinking about religion that we are here proposing a new word seems appropriate, so we suggest poiesis, a suitable term for the age of linguistic philosophy. It means a making or a creation, and in particular linguistic creation, the art of poetry. So it is the right term to be used by people who see linguistic creation as producing all other sorts of change.

Religion differs from art in being more directly communal and ethical. It has a stronger social responsibility, because it has to be positive. It must affirm that nihilism can be conquered and that our life together can be made meaningful and worthwhile. So religion has the positive 'political' task of finding ever-new metaphors under which our life can be viewed and made to appear newly-meaningful, and of finding new good causes – that is, things currently undervalued that can be upgraded to the general benefit. Religion must always strive to be affirmative and social, whereas great art may very well sometimes find itself being blasphemously negative, nihilistic and antisocial. When that is so, then religion needs to find a way of incorporating that negative moment into the movement of its own language. It should do so unreservedly, but its last word needs to be affirmative. Thus a religious exegete may try to demonstrate something noble, a certain movement of resignation and reconciliation, in the closing scenes of King Lear. But the exegesis must be good exegesis. When we insist that religion has a positive social duty to generate myths and symbols that will make life seem worth living and to raise valuations so that we all have something to live for, we do not mean that there is any excuse for encouraging consoling illusions or perpetuating lies.

Religion, then, is a sort of communal poetry by which our life comes forth into expression as meaningful and valuable. There has of course been a long tradition of discussions of analogy, symbolism and metaphor which has been largely concerned with whether and how human words are able to refer to and even, just a little, *describe* things divine and supernatural. But that is not a profitable line of enquiry. More important is the question of how signs are able to attract and express libido, and thereby to create and structure reality.

Notice that on our view there is no purely biological level of human life, prior to its expression in the sign. Our human life is significant or sign-formed all the way down, so that to speak of a particular cultural or religious system as 'a form of life' and to speak of it as 'a regime of signs' is to say the same thing. A sign is a feeling expressed as a meaning.

3. The sign

How then does the sign work? How is it able to excite libido and lure it forward into structured and world-creating expression? Jung uses the formula, 'Symbols attract and transmute libido', but is not very clear about just how this happens. The most extreme and interesting case is that of the fashion business. Why is it that this year (1989) sunglasses had to be so round and goggly, and why is it that next year the fashion imperative will have changed? Why is it that this year the white leather trainer-style half boots worn by one tribe of the young had to be so very white, with such gaudy decorative features and such high tongues? Why is it that certain shapes and colours turn on the trendy, and not just some but all of them; and why is it that just what turns them on has to be different each season?

Although we have no full theory, an outline formal theory of fashion can be very easily stated. Three main points need to be made. The first, from standard psychoanalytical doctrine, recommends us to begin by thinking of libido as vague, malleable and easily trained or displaced.[9] Libido cannot express itself, cannot emerge, until it has got a form to flow into. Libido needs to be seduced. It is never preformed, but must wait for culture to switch it on by offering it an enticing path to take.[10] Hence the possibility of very diverse special forms, tastes, orientations or fetishes. In the slang, my current taste is what I am just now 'into'. In the past culture has turned libido into sanctity, militarism, high fashion and great art with equal ease.

Secondly, like many other animals we are so constituted that we respond very quickly and strongly to movement, change and difference, whereas even a pleasurable sensation soon becomes dulled if it does not vary. As a result, while it is true that libido is always a little fixated, in that there is always some particular symbolic form by which it is most excited and through which it likes to flow, just what it is currently 'into' must always be shifting a little.

If both stimulus and response (that is, both the sign and the libidinal expression it facilitates) were fully specific, human behaviour would be rigid and incapable of unforced change. Fortunately, our physiology is so constituted as to permit a certain bandwidth of variation both in the qualities of the stimulus and in the strength of the response. This is called generality or 'stimulus generalization', and it has a dual beneficial consequence: on the one hand generality makes it possible for our behaviour to drop into regular patterns and become describable and in some measure reliable, while on the other hand the same generality provides a little play or flexibility, which makes it possible for our behaviour patterns to develop in an unforced way. As in the case of the chromosomes at the time of sexual reproduction, what is needed is a neat trade-off between reliable replication and a possibility of innovation. And that we have.

Thirdly, we human beings are highly sociable, and therefore compete vigorously and enjoyably to be the most intelligent, sensitive, trendy and quick on the uptake. Everybody wants to be upfront, close to the place where it is at. This is as true of the most abstract philosophy as it is of the fashion in sunglasses. When in 1911 Wittgenstein became intensely interested in the philosophy of mathematics he wanted to know where it was at. He quickly discovered the answer. He saw Frege in Vienna and Russell at Cambridge, and became the latter's pupil. The ablest people just do gravitate irresistibly towards the rainbow's end, the magic spot from which, for the moment, it is all beginning. Perhaps because Plato left us with the notion that the loftiest pursuits are concerned with timeless matters, we still have a certain reluctance to admit that the laws of fashion apply to them in full. But they do. Histories of religious devotion or of religious art show it.[11] Perhaps the best single example is the summit of Christian art in Northern France in the thirteenth century, marked by ultra-rapid development, furious excess, expense, energy and enthusiasm, and almost instant diffusion of the new style through neighbouring countries. If ever there was a fashionable craze, the French Gothic was it.

The great achievements in art, thought and religion come from the periods when people are competing most fiercely to be the first and set the tone.

So we have at least the outline of a general theory of fashion and cultural change. Libido must have symbolic forms in which to express itself, and indeed just isn't there at all until it has got a form within which it can emerge. The sign produces libido by seducing it, turns it on and gives it expression. Secondly though, to maintain the flow of libido, the sign must move. There must be development and change, or we get stuck in a rut. Thirdly, because we are all so sociable we all move together, keeping as close as we can get to the magical and often very elusive source from which the fashion originates.

This very general account explains why in every area of human life there is always a fashion, which is always social, which has leaders, which must continually change, and which is essential just to keep life going. Freud was inclined to a certain biologism, and talked as if libido might exist as a biological force before culture comes along and offers it a symbolic form through which it can express itself. But I argue that we can have no access to the thing itself prior to and independent of its entry into the world of signs. There isn't any 'natural man'. A human being is social all the way down. From the very first libido is already formed and given symbolic meaning by culture. Life and language are co-extensive. The movement of signs is the process of life itself, the continual creation of the world.

However, the account I have given has done nothing at all to explain just why it has to be round goggly sunglasses that are compulsory his year, whereas next year perhaps we will have to buy strongly horizontal wrap-around shades such as might be worn by racing drivers. Why is this? Undoubtedly round goggly sunglasses are sexy this year, but we don't necessarily have to find any quasi-biological explanation of why this should be so. It is quite possible for libido to be socially trained to respond to an 'unmotivated' or arbitrary sign. So it could be that many of the contingent details of what happens to be fashionable this year are not in themselves significant. The point is rather that the entire business of fashion, its movement and its irresistible imperatives, is itself a symbolic system. The more preposterous the dictates of fashion and the more powerful its sway, the more obvious it becomes that fashion is about something other than itself. What? The key is that it usually emanates from a group of people who are described as being in a special and strong sense 'Society', and by our strenuous efforts to keep up with it we demonstrate our own loyalty to society.

Again, why? Because the most important sign-system is not fashion in dress, but language. And human life cannot function at all unless we are all of us both strictly loyal to the rules of our language, and also ultra-sensitive to the ways in which meanings are all the time changing. People may smile at the teenager who is a slave to fashion, but her behaviour, I am suggesting, is sym-bolic. We must all of us be like that if language is to work. Unless we keep ourselves very finely attuned to the common language, we will soon become unable by what we say to mean anything at

all. That's the modern version of Kant's doctrine that objectivity
in our knowledge depends upon certain necessary truths. To
demythologize Kant, translate: for objectivity read public intelligibility, and for necessary truths read social imperatives. The
resolution of the old struggle between freedom and determinism
then takes the new form of a proof that only through strict con-
formity to the currently-established rules of language can I
produce anything of my own that is intelligible to others. More-
over, it is only through society that I can become intelligible even
to myself. There is no power-to-mean inside me that is independent of society. In the older tradition, of which Husserl was one
of the last representatives, people seem to have believed they had
non-linguistic thoughts. They seem to have supposed that by a
personal act of intending they could somehow force a personal
meaningfulness into their own utterances, and that by a private
speechless act of intending they could even make their own
thoughts meaningful to themselves. But this was an illusion. Our
inner thoughts, such as they are, are interiorizations of speech and
so depend for their sense upon the public language. And our
utterances mean nothing until they mean something to others, so
that again I am not able personally to control what is meant by
what I say. What is meant by what I say is a public matter, and
not one over which I the speaker have any special authority. So
we have to acknowledge that society precedes the individual. If in
the fashion business we see individuals rather absurdly constrained
by an ever-changing regime of almost-comically arbitrary signs,
well, that is the human condition, for that is how language and
culture constrain us all.

Now we have to ask how this regime of signs produces the
world we live in. Undoubtedly there is a sharp conflict at this
point between traditional realists, who put Nature before Culture
and therefore start with material objectivity and then move in-
wards, and anti-realists who tend to move outwards from language
to reality. And equally certainly, most English speakers remain
Aristotelians, instinctive realists about sense-experience, about the
life-world, about scientific theory and about religious objects. A

striking example is Richard Swinburne, who suggests that

> ... it is a principle of rationality that (in the absence of special considerations) if it seems (epistemically) to a subject that x is present, then probably x is present; what one seems to perceive is probably so.[12]

By the same token,

> ... all religious experiences ought to be taken by their subjects as genuine, and hence as substantial grounds for belief in the existence of their apparent object ...[13]

This principle Swinburne engagingly calls the Principle of Credulity. He thinks that we will be landed in a 'sceptical bog' if we do not accept it in respect of everyday secular experiences, and he does not see any sufficient reason for not accepting it in the case of religious experiences, too. He takes the bull by the horns:

> ... sceptics are apt to deny the claim of some Portuguese peasant to have seen Mary, on the grounds that the description which the peasant gives of the way Mary was dressed does not fit the way Mary used to dress in Palestine, but closely corresponds to the way she is pictured on the walls of Portuguese churches. That seems to me to count not at all against the peasant's claim. For if Mary has survived death, what reason is there to suppose that she now has to dress the way she did in Palestine? If she is to manifest herself in bodily form the obvious way for her to dress is the way in which she would be recognized by those to whom she appears.[14]

Clearly Swinburne is not going to be dislodged from this position by mere epidemiological facts about visions of Mary. If we ask why she appears only to Catholic and Orthodox Christians, how she knows the local language, and why she nowadays appears mainly in peasant regions and not to middle-class Catholics, Swinburne can just keep replying, why not? The philosophical disagreement between him and the anti-realist evidently goes a long way back. And I am inclined to agree with Swinburne that in this matter religious and secular experiences are on the same footing. For the realist, it is a principle of rationality that unless we have good grounds to think otherwise we should start from the presumption that things are what they seem to be. In particular, if Catholics are having visions of Mary then we should start from the presumption that Mary is appearing to them. For the anti-realist, the reason why Catholics and only Catholics are having visions of Mary is simply that they are Catholics. The religious symbol-system you live by evokes and structures your religious experience, just as quite generally the common language structures our ordinary experience of the world. We can see what we can describe. So the realist and the anti-realist can each explain the phenomena. To each party in this dispute her own position seems so obvious that it takes something like a religious conversion to get a realist across to the anti-realist point of view. (Conversion, in this particular case, goes in one direction only. Anti-realists do not revert to realism.)

It is not easy to find arguments for anti-realism that are acceptable to the realist by her own criteria. But Swinburne does acknowledge that superior explanatory power is a weighty consideration. By that criterion, the anti-realist wins. Looking at the whole history of the Mary-cult in its historical context, and showing the part that they have played in that history, the anti-realist explains why visions of Mary occur when and where they do, and why they take the form they do. Visions of Mary are products of Catholicism, and as such can be adequately explained by the usual methods of historical explanation. By contrast, Swinburne's realist view of visions of Mary has the familiar faults of all supernaturalist explanations – it postulates numerous incomprehensible occult goings-on, and explains nothing at all. The appearance of bluff English commonsense cannot be sustained. Suppose, for example, that we were politely to request Swinburne to fill in a few of the missing details for us by explaining just how Mary selects the people she is going to appear to, in what heavenly language lab she learns Portuguese of the right century and in the right local dialect, and so on; then, whether Swinburne obligingly supplies a full answer or refuses one, either way, it will be shown that no explanation of his type can be made tolerably clear and full while remaining sensible. By contrast, the anti-realist sort of explanation can be supported by abundant psychological data, case-histories and the like, illustrating the manifold ways in which visions and hallucinations are shaped by culture and by the psychology of the experient. And of course those who write histories of the Middle Ages have no difficulty in weaving into their narratives visions, miracles and the like, understood in the normal anti-realist way as expressions of the culture of the period; whereas a would-be historian of the Middle Ages who attempted to include in his narrative realistically-interpreted visions and miracles, and the action of supernatural causes generally, wouldn't actually succeed in writing history at all. He would be writing a kind of science fiction or fantasy.

There are a number of other arguments for anti-realism which may have some weight with realists. Anti-realism does not say that there is no world at all, but only that we cannot compare our view of the world with the way the world is absolutely, for we have no access to the way things are absolutely. So we are stuck with our view of the world, which is theory-laden. I see everything around me in the light of scientific theories, most of them of quite recent origin. H. G. Wells, amazingly as it seems now, could still postulate life on the moon. He must have seen a rather different moon from the one we see. But people of different periods live in different worlds, and from the anti-realist point of view it makes perfect sense to regard all knowledge as historically-produced, and to say that the world of the Middle Ages was a different world from the modern world.

Nor is there anything in the least far-fetched about the anti-realist view that the world is produced within language. Look out of the window with me at the garden. The instant your eye lights upon it, the words *tree*, *green*, *willow* and so on make you see a tree. What Plato calls Forms and Kant calls concepts, I call just words, and I am saying that since we have all of us been inducted into language, we function in words. We look, the looking instantly activates the general words *tree, green, willow* etc. – and now we see. So the words are constitutive of the experience, and the whole surface of the world is covered over with words (or signs, to use a slightly wider term). It is in that sense that there is only language. Realists seem to think they have only to say, 'That's a weeping willow by the pond out there', and the sentence will fly out of the window, wrap itself tightly round its referent, and then evaporate, leaving us locked unmistakably on to the un-interpreted thing itself. But I say the world *stays* blanketted-over with language, and that this interpretative blanketting changes over time, is different in different cultures and so on. So different people(s) see different worlds. All of which is entirely in accord with everyday experience. Yes, the world you see depends upon the vocabulary you've got and upon any special knowledge you've got. Yes, perceptions of reality differ, and often the world seems to be a writhing tangle of conflicting interpretations. Yes, both on the individual scale and on the larger cultural scale our view of the world is a reflection of and therefore a judgment upon what we are. And yes, by changing our vocabulary we can change the valuations of things, and so can change our world. That is all just commonsense, because anti-realism is now the view of the world most consistent with commonsense.

If signs structure all our experience of the world, and if the movement of signs is the movement of life itself, what makes a sign a *religious* sign? The question is important because we refuse the traditional 'platonic' view of the religious sign. The religious sign does not refer to something transcendent; it is not a window upon eternity, and it is not to be seen as sublimating libido and redirecting it towards a higher world. Our view is resolutely one-level or 'naturalistic'. Human life coincides with the movement of the world of signs as a whole, and has no outside. The whole system of signs is a moving continuum like the sea. So our account does not permit the establishment of a distinct and unchanging religious realm. Evidently we need to say how on a view like ours there can be religious signs at all, and what they are.

The question cannot be answered empirically in the Jungian

manner by undertaking (or purporting to undertake) a comprehensive survey of all the religions of the world, and then cataloguing and classifying all their signs. The material is too overwhelming, and the general classification of it – since it must attempt to override the local contextualization of each sign – will always and unavoidably be a falsification.

So we proceed instead philosophically. Religious signs are a special and anomalous group of signs. They are signs of signs. Through the way they are manipulated in religion we are enabled to get a kind of overview of our life (i.e., of the whole movement of the world of signs), and be reconciled to it. So the religious sign does not point out of the world altogether, as was commonly suggested in the older mythical-platonic philosophies of religion, but instead refreshes our vision of the world by turning us around full circle. We see things a little more clearly, and in a way that helps to cure us of fretfulness, egoism, fear and discontent.

Religious signs are then signs of signs, and for there to be a productive ritual movement or dialectical play among them they need to be of three sorts: signs of life, signs of death, and signs of the Whole, or eternal life. We associate these three sorts of signs with the colours red, black and white.

The red signs, the signs of Life, are signs of signs that function to heighten our awareness of the way the pulse, the equivocality and the nervous tension of life are expressed in all signs. So the signs of Life are associated with the heart, rhythmic pulsation, blood, danger, ordeal, sexual excitement, warfare and whatever else attracts our attention, puts us to the test, makes our sensibility quiver, and enhances life's awareness of itself.

The black signs, the signs of Death, are anomalous in the sense that although they are generated and move within the world of signs, they are symbols of the negation of the whole moving world of signs as such. They are like the zero in mathematics. And if every sign is an expression of life, how can there be signs of death unless libido itself is dialectical, so that we do indeed sometimes catch ourselves yearning for death, otherness, difference and the Void? Both in sexual desire and in religious yearnings there is a strand that seeks self-loss in absolute otherness. We know we must die eventually, and we are intensely curious to know what it will be like to be dead. So life seeks a kind of anticipatory and symbolic knowledge of what death is, and thereby a reflexively enhanced awareness of itself, through erotic and religious self-surrender. The signs of death express, then, life's movement towards its own Other.

The white signs, the signs of Eternal Life, which may also be blue or gold, are anomalous in that they are signs of the whole world of signs, a Whole that cannot be achieved and is seemingly impossible. The signs of the Whole reconcile life and death, continual motion and motionlessness, and the untotalizable ambiguity and secondariness of the world of signs in which we are immersed with a complete, perfected and radiant Whole. The opposites are briefly, impossibly, united and we say a wholehearted Yes to life.

Religious rituals are, roughly, literary texts. They lead us from Life through Death to Eternal Life. As the sign-movement involved becomes habitual to us and in us, so we become gradually happier and better people. The message of religion is simple. At present metaphysical delusions, moral wickedness and emotional stress and discontent darken our life, making our world ugly and ourselves wretched. We have to die and be reborn, a rebirth through which not only we but also our world will be recreated. We must encounter, accept and be de-centred and transformed by otherness, difference and death. Through that experience our vision of our situation will be refreshed and clarified. Eternal happiness is to love life enough to give ourselves completely to it in the present moment. It is to be absorbed in love and work.

This message of salvation by a symbolic progression from life through death to eternal life is further elaborated in religious myths such as that of the life, death and resurrection of Jesus. Of which more later.

4. Nothing final

Profoundly different mentalities co-exist among us. So long as the talk runs only upon everyday matters, we may get along without difficulty. But when questions of ethics, religion and philosophy arise, chasms open. We realize that other people construct their worlds in entirely different ways and out of quite different materials.

I suggest that we find three main groups. Traditional realists make their universe out of beings, critical realists make their world of knowledge, and anti-realists live in a world of language.

The traditional realists comprise the majority of religious believers and a very wide range of members of the public who, although they are no longer themselves believers, still find the traditional language of belief perfectly intelligible. Such people can quite straightforwardly ask, 'Is there a God?' and, 'Do we have souls?' The existence-questions come first. The answers to these questions may indeed vary, but all realists think in terms of establishing what is out there. In both religion and philosophy we need to orient ourselves towards and be guided by what is most real. It seems natural to think that what is most real is also greatest in power and perfection, and has the right to lay down the Law.

The difficulty we find in debate with a person who thinks like this is that he effectively equates realism in philosophy with piety in religion. The philosophy seems to be telling us first to identify our correct place in the order of beings, and then to be guided by the Supreme Being, so that it is very difficult to question it without attracting very intense religious opprobrium. Philosophy says realism is piety, and then religion adopts and defends that thesis. Religion says, 'Don't you dare deny that what is most real must be worshipped, and what is worshipped must be most real!' To the outsider the religion may seem to be functioning as a fierce watchdog, guarding what is basically a philosophical doctrine. But to the insider, piety and realism seem quite inseparable. He will not allow a wedge to be driven between the two.

The critical realists comprise the great majority of scientists, critical historians and others whose world effectively consists of the organized body of 'our' critically tested and communally agreed knowledge. For them the known is the real. They are apt to deride the ontology of the traditional realists. 'What do you mean?', they will ask, 'How do you know? Where is your evidence, and what are your checking-procedures?' Critical realists are not particularly concerned with truth-as-correspondence – or at least, need not be so concerned. What they *are* passionately concerned about is the idea of a science; the objectivity and the strength of a body of knowledge developed by a rigorous method, and at every point open to testing by procedures that can be publicly specified, applied and assessed.

The third group, the anti-realists, are often people whose chief interest lies in society, history and the humanities, in language, interpretation and rhetoric rather than in being or knowledge. Anti-realists watch the words that people use and the games that people play. They see the world as being like a literary text, full of linguistic ploys and stratagems, and endlessly discussable, and they secretly regard science as being naive in its one-eyed objectivism. They don't quite believe in existence or facts, for they see the world as made of signs, fictions and interpretations. Like some camp Catholics, they greatly enjoy religious ritual and symbolism, but they cannot regard the doctrinal side of religion as anything but mythical, or perhaps as a tool of power.

At this point the gap in understanding can be hilarious. The puritan believer and the scientist are at one in their commitment to unity and univocity, personal integrity, objective truth, and deep-down rigour and system. As they see it the anti-realist is a deeply repugnant person who believes only in frippery – externals, the play of appearances, plurality and deception. So far as the serious business of ontology and knowledge is concerned, the anti-realist would seem to be a complete sceptic or perhaps a Buddhist. He or she doesn't really believe anything at all, because of course, there isn't really any 'real'.

Now in these matters the view you get depends on the direction in which you are moving. But many, many of us are former platonists, puritans and Cartesians. We have moved from traditional realism through critical realism and are now well into anti-realism, so that we seem to ourselves to have lost everything, to have gone into and through the Nihil, and to have emerged blinking into a world which (like this, the present text) is made only of the ever-changing play of human language. If we had travelled in some other direction things might have looked different, but we have come *this* way and so things look as they do.

The outcome is highly paradoxical, because our journey has led to the loss of all the assumptions underlying the metaphor of life as a journey. Because the play of linguistic meaning and interpretation is endless, indeed just because of the very simple idea that meaning is historically-produced and is differential, the whole idea of a Final Truth out there which at the Last Day will be reached by us and get stated in language has broken down. Our journey has taught us to give up the notion of life as a journey, quest, search or pilgrimage, because it rests upon the objectivist illusion of a Truth out there. We have unlearnt that idea of Truth: truth as a magic formula, a hidden secret of life. Our conclusion has been that there is no conclusion. Any sense there is, we make and must keep on remaking. It is a mistake to dream of a Final Cosmic Interpretation so stupendously plonking that it leaves no more to be said, completely satisfies everyone and shuts us all up forever, for if it were stated in any vocabulary that we could understand there would always be room for arguments about how to interpret it, and it would inevitably be open to dispute.

Three consequences of all this must be pointed out at once. First, every sort of social utopianism has broken down, and in fact there occurred around the 1960s a fairly general collapse of the master-narratives telling of the assured progress of mankind towards universal liberation or redemption.[15] Secondly, if it no longer makes sense to justify life in the present by appealing to the promise of a glorious future, then we must find the meaning of life in the way in which we ourselves relate ourselves to life in the present moment. We must do it *Now*, because things are not going to get better than they are now. And thirdly, any faith or philosophy of life that we adopt will be only a script. It cannot wholly relieve us of the responsibility for living our own lives, for we shall still have to find our own interpretation of it and to put on our own performance of it. If history changes truth, if there are no fixed essences, meanings or truths, then we must make things up as we go along. As members of a group we will have a common vocabulary, but each of us will have to find our own voice in it.

The old theme of the creation of the world now takes on a new aspect. The traditional distinctions between the First Cause and second causes, and between the Creation of the world 'in the beginning' and the subsequent process of things, disappear. Creation becomes the moment by moment process of life, which is also the movement of language from sign to sign. The process of creation flows through us.

In this way the endless productivity of language and interpretation, which dissolved away the earlier systems of thought and led to the crisis of nihilism, now itself becomes the starting-point for a new order. In religion in particular, we lost the old idea of orienting ourselves towards and being guided by an objective reality and Truth of things out there, but we gain instead a new idea of religion as our relation to the ceaseless bubbling-up of language and interpretation within us by which our life is continually reinvented and renewed. 'I am convinced that God hath more light yet to break out of his Holy Word', said a Protestant sailing to America long ago. Similarly, we say that no limit can be set beforehand to the things we may yet find it possible to do with the vocabulary we have received from the past.

IV

A THEORY OF GOD

1. Religious naturalism

Can anything be done at this time of day to clear up the confusion surrounding the words 'God', 'religion' and 'atheism'? One may well doubt it. Our literary tradition will not go away. It shows how fiercely contested these words have been throughout the four millennia or so of which we have record.[1] Each new group that comes into the ascendant redefines the terms in its own interest. As a result, the words 'God', 'true religion' and 'atheism' have been pushed around so much that they have frequently changed places, or have been used in diametrically opposite ways by opposing parties. For example, an intellectual who rejects the gods of popular religion and accepts only the God of rationalist philosophy may be called an atheist by some in some contexts. Yet there is also the exactly contrary case of the sceptic who rejects metaphysics, declares for a form of fideistic commitment to the God of popular religion – and gets called an atheist by the philosophers. Still more obviously political is the case of the religious iconoclast who attacks the established state cult as idolatrous. Here there will be a straightforward tussle between the dissident and the official defenders of the state religion, as each tries to pin the label of atheist upon the other. The historical record indicates that in religion more than anywhere else, alas, truth has depended on power. Victory confers linguistic rights, and those who win ensure that everything gets labelled the way they want it to be.

113

Some of the greatest controversies over the word 'God' have never been settled, and it is hard to see how they ever could be. Consider the issue between the rationalists and the voluntarists, whom we may imagine as being typified by, for example, Spinoza and Calvin. The rationalist argues that we human beings are unhappy because we are ignorant and at the mercy of external forces. We lack understanding, and feel distanced from God and from ourselves. The only way for us to achieve human perfection is by a rigorous deduction of our unity with the one self-subsistent divine totality, God or Nature, of which we are modes. On this account, then, the religious interest itself requires that God and our unity with him must be perfectly comprehended by reason and made fully transparent. However, the voluntarist reacts with horror to this conclusion (and of course Spinoza has very often been called an atheist). Religion, on the alternative account, requires a God with the power to save us, which means a God who is transcendent over the world, sovereign, free and incomprehensible. As the old slogan has it: 'God understood is not God.' So one party claims that if human beings are to achieve eternal happiness God must be perfectly understood by reason, whereas the other party says precisely the opposite. And nobody can find, or will ever find, the Archimedean point from which it could really be determined which of these views we would do best to follow. The dispute is endless. The two positions in question are both so stupendously grand that we would not even wish either of them to be wiped off the map. We actually prefer pluralism.

'But that is an horrific position to maintain!', it will be declared. 'You are saying that you would rather keep the intellectual pleasure to be got from contemplating the endless clash of opposed views than discover one of them to be right and gain your salvation through it. You actually *prefer* pluralism and intellectual aestheticism to salvation by the Truth!'

Yes indeed, because we are Westerners and not Muslims. My problem is – and perhaps it is yours, too – that although I profess to love truth I could not actually endure a One-Truth universe, because even as the angels ushered me into Heaven I would still be nourishing the suspicion that it was all trumped-up, an illusion created by power. I sincerely believe that I would rather contemplate the conflict of two great truths and feel I had a choice between them, because that possibility of choice disperses power a little. A Christian is a peculiar sort of monotheist who unexpectedly likes powerlessness. I would really rather have both Calvin and Spinoza, and the chance to debate the great issue between them, than wipe out one of them, know the other was True, and be saved. You are the same, probably, so it sounds as if we Westerners actually prefer and have chosen the nihilism that has engulfed us. We gave up Truth and sold our souls, all for freedom's sake.

That seems to mean that we must also accept the resulting endless contestation of God, true religion and atheism. We'd rather have moveable meanings than Meaning fixed by Power. If we can move meanings we have a little freedom, a little room to make a truth of our own in our own lives.

The price to be paid is that we must learn to live with intellectual pluralism, which is not easy. How are we to cope with this? One way is to go historical. We try to write a genealogy of the present; we re-mind ourselves of our tradition. There have been a number of very good surveys of what has happened to God in the thought of the past few centuries.[2] They tend to follow Heidegger in writing a story of decline. In the twelfth and thirteenth centuries, we are told, our culture was still in pretty good shape and people knew what God is and what religion is. But what with Protestantism, the secular nation-state, the Enlightenment and so on, Western thought has been wandering ever-further off course. So in the closing pages of the book Western thought finds itself being duly shepherded back along the path to the Catholic fold. There was a hidden agenda after all. Nor is this anything to complain about, because the work would not have been readable unless it had had some kind of story to tell which shaped the choice of characters and the way they were treated. Nevertheless, we learn that panoramic histories showing the interplay of a vast range of points of view upon God must themselves have a point of view – which means there can be any number of them. History is good at showing the sheer extent of the problem, especially if we read several histories from different angles; but it can contribute nothing to the solution.

An alternative to writing history-of-ideas about God is the method adopted by many philosophers and theologians. They simply offer a definition of God, sometimes saying that they hope they are right in supposing that this is what the tradition says, or what most people think. Then they try to establish whether or not there exists a being answering to their definition. The procedure is oddly *a priori*, and pays scant attention either to the history of religions, or to the social-psychology evidence about what most people think, or to any lessons that are to be learnt from the prolonged debate in the modern West. At any rate, its results have been disappointing.

There is another and relatively-unexplored possibility. Why not try as coolly as possible to *explain* belief in God, in a way that would do as much justice as we can to the evidence of its very long history, vast diversity, fiercely-contested character and so on? Such an explanation will have to be naturalistic in order to count as an explanation, so that even when it tries hard to be cool it will inevitably attract accusations of prejudice. However, it may be able to prove its value by taking account of a wider range of evidence than its most powerful rivals, the mainstream theologies. We may even be led to the conclusion that religious naturalism is *religiously* superior to the traditional supernaturalist theologies.

How could this come about? On the traditional supernaturalist account our religious beliefs are more important to us than anything else, and therefore have to be dogmatically and realistically just True. Everything other than the Truth is not merely a harmless mistake but an actively pernicious delusion. But all major religions are internally divided, and even the biggest of them embraces only a minority of the human race. Supernatural theologies must then hold that most human beings in all ages have been in the grip of damnable and damning illusions, a view difficult to reconcile with God's universal power and love; whereas from the standpoint of religious naturalism the religions are cultural constructions which need not be seen as directly contradicting each other. There is plenty of room for many faiths to be valuable, and for many to coexist amicably in our modern multifaith societies. We are not religiously obliged to attempt to stamp out other religions.

The superiority of religious naturalism is perhaps most obvious in relation to the problem of evil, to which we have already referred (II.7). The point can be put very shortly: we cannot say why the God of Israel should have permitted the Holocaust to happen, but we can say for sure that only because of their religion have the Jews been able to survive as a people. That is, where the problem of evil is concerned the old supernatural theologies are always on the defensive, struggling against hopeless odds, whereas religious naturalism has the better of the argument all along. Obviously supernaturalism has no 'answer' to the problem of evil, but equally obviously religion, understood as a human cultural institution, helps societies to resist and survive evil. It gives people hope and the will to live. It unites people around shared myths and values. While they cling to it, people have something to live for.

Religious naturalism is also better able to explain the diversity of religious belief. Gods are national; they embody cultural values. That is why the Indian gods, the Greek gods and the Egyptian gods differ. People speak of a Russian God and of a Jewish God. They say, 'Show me your God, and I'll tell you who you are.' That is, on the naturalistic view our central and identity-defining values and myths are expressed in our religious beliefs. On the naturalistic view what matters is not whether or not a God exists, but rather, what *kind* of God you believe in – that is, what values and what myths are authoritative for you. Notoriously a realistic theist has got real problems in explaining the sense in which the God of Israel, of Christianity, and of Islam really is still one and the same Only True God, when the three faiths have diverged so much. What can survive of the old idea of a revelation by God of his own nature – that is, God's telling us what he's really like and what values he really stands for – when the members of three successive faiths in the same tradition of revelation have come to differ so greatly from each other? On the naturalistic view, just history – that is, just the historical development of cultural and moral traditions – can explain the fact that by now the God of Islam has become a very different character from the God of Christians and also from the God of Jews. On the naturalistic view our gods do not have objectively-fixed and permanent identities. They are simply what *we* postulate them as being. And religion changes. So there is no difficulty in acknowledging that the *de facto* God of modern Christianity has become very different from the God of sixteenth-century Christianity. But such historical development of the moral content of religious belief, though it obviously happens, is very difficult to reconcile with the old view that an objective God once gave us a final revelation of what he is really and timelessly like. If he did, why are our theologies so historically-conditioned and so easily datable? Why did we change God as we manifestly have done, if in fact God is unchangeable?

A further argument arises at this point. Because the older supernatural theology saw itself as in some sense describing a God who existed unchangeably outside religious language, it projected the truth of its own doctrines back to the beginnings of humanity. Thus the doctrine of the Trinity was read back into *Genesis*. There was no clear idea of the evolution of religion, and some people continued to believe in primitive monotheism, as it was called, until the present century.[3] Yet in retrospect it is now clear that human beings could not have believed in One God until they had reasonably unified notions of the cosmos, of the human self, and of control both over society and over Nature. Until those ideas were available, there were no metaphors through which the One Creator-God could be spoken of. So the idea of God has and must have had a human history. It became possible to us only when our language about ourselves and our world had reached a certain level of development. In fact the idea of God represents a great victory, an early-historical anticipation of the Enlightenment, because it shows human beings becoming able to conceive of a full and unifying knowledge and control of themselves, their world and their history. Religious naturalism can understand and accept all this; but supernaturalism has difficulties.

Finally, standard theologies often do not do very well even on their own home ground. They may claim to systematize, to interpret or to explain 'the data of revelation', while yet in practice their actual performance is very erratic and poor. Perhaps the problem has been that they have simply not been challenged enough. The obvious questions have not been asked. To repeat an earlier-quoted example, Christian theologies do not explain why the most intense and vivid expression of God in the Bible is to be found not in the New Testament, where God seems to have largely faded away, but in the canonical prophets of Israel, and perhaps also in Exodus. If the supreme revelation of God is in Jesus Christ, why is it that in the texts of the prophets from Amos to Jeremiah God is so very much more intense, vivid, close and overwhelming than ever he is in the recorded teaching of Jesus? Perhaps the question can be answered; but it first needs to be asked, and so far it has not been.

I am suggesting then that just as supernaturalist ways of thinking have been expelled from all the natural and social sciences, chiefly because they just don't explain things very well, so also it is about time they were expelled from religion. Supernatural theologies cannot cope with the problem of evil, cannot on their own premisses explain the vast diversity of religions and their human history, and do not even do a very good job of explaining the contents of their own scriptures. So there is plenty of scope for religious naturalism to do a better job of explaining religion and showing why it always has mattered and still matters so much to us. In this way religious naturalism might come to be thought more religiously-adequate than the old supernatural theologies were.

Unfortunately, cool and genuinely wide-ranging religious naturalism has so far been uncommon. There have been three main traditions, but none that has been wholly satisfactory.

There is, first, an irregular and idiosyncratic line of Western thinkers, going back to presocratic times, who have put forward naturalistic interpretations of religion. Modern figures in this tradition have included Spinoza, Feuerbach, Marx, Freud, Durkheim, Jung and Julian Jaynes. Few of them were very cool. Some were militantly anti-religious, while others claimed to be sympathetic fellow-travellers. But all of them have the air of farewell-theorists who have left the communal practice of any religion well behind them.

Overlapping a little with those names, there are the four or five main schools of thought about how to interpret religion and ritual that have prevailed among anthropologists.[4] They include intellectualism, symbolism, functionalism and structuralism. (Claude Lévi-Strauss might have been listed with those named in the previous paragraph, but it seems likely that structuralism as a method and a school of thought in the social sciences will prove more durable than Lévi-Strauss's own structural technique of myth-interpretation.) Here again, though, the anthropologists' theories of religion are on the whole farewell-theories. They do little to suggest what sort of continuing importance religion may yet have in the most advanced societies. Sometimes, as in the case of Durkheim, the effect of the anthropologists' theories is nihilistic, for the moves by which the theorist shows the constitutive role of religion in traditional societies simultaneously rule it out for us. If you understand Durkheim's theory of religion, you understand both that religion was once essential, and that it is now out of your reach, just because you understand it.

Finally, there is the line of American pragmatists and radical empiricists stemming from James, Dewey and the Chicago School, a hundred-year tradition of religious naturalism that still survives in the American Academy of Religion and in some university Schools of Religion.[5] It is a tradition of ultra-liberal protestantism which tends to demythologize faith into trust in life, a positive attitude to life, an aesthetic response to our life-world as a whole, commitment to a God who symbolizes communal values and so on. As such it has done something to explain the sense in which a modern person may still have a religious attitude to life, but it does not as yet offer a very convincing biography of God. It does not explain why God is so prodigiously eloquent in Amos, Hosea and the others, but has since fallen silent and progressively faded away. Only Julian Jaynes has produced a clear theory on that particular point.

In summary, religious naturalism deserves further investigation. It might lead to a theory of religion superior to that embodied in the usual supernatural theologies. It has already a remarkable and varied history and some great names. But it has not yet fulfilled its promise.

2. The God of speech

If religious naturalism is to produce a new and interesting theory of God it must begin by noting certain features of the idea of God which for over two millennia have been relatively unnoticed, or even systematically excluded from attention, by the literary traditions of philosophy and theology. The reason for this long exclusion will appear later.

First, then, the entire philosophical tradition at least up to Hegel, and followed by orthodox theology, has tended to locate God in a universal and timeless realm beyond language and society. The God of the philosophers in particular is (or purports to be) thereby dissociated from any special relationship with a cultural tradition. But this diverts attention away from the fact that all notions of God are in practice highly culture-specific and fiercely contested. A people's God is always proper to them, at the heart of their culture, being the vehicle of their traditional values and the basis of their ethnic identity. In Bronze-Age and even early Iron-Age times, battles between peoples were represented as battles between their gods. A god's job was to fight for his people, so that a victory for Israel was naturally a victory for the God of Israel, Yahweh. The same was true for other peoples.

In our more recent post-traditional societies the idea of God is less highly communal. Each individual in some measure frames a personal concept of God, a concept which is highly informative about the person whose god this is. Your god is (amongst other things, no doubt) an expression of your values, what you live by and what you aspire after. But although this may sound like the teaching of Ludwig Feuerbach, there is an important difference. Whether consistently or not, Feuerbach still believed in a human essence, the concrete universal 'Man' or 'Humanity'; and because he thus believed in one standard human nature, Feuerbach followed the philosophical tradition in believing also in one universal and common God – albeit, as the alienated objectification of the universal human essence. We disagree with Feuerbach in that for us there is no longer any one enduring and transhistorical human essence. (For example, it is now widely admitted that ideas of what it is to be a woman have varied considerably in different cultures in the past, and that what a woman *really* is and should be is not an essence given to us *a priori*, but rather is something that women are going to have to invent and keep on reinventing for themselves in the future. And the same is therefore presumably true for men also.) But if there is no one timelessly authoritative human essence to tell us what we really are, then there is not going to be any one privileged, universal and timeless definition of God either, whether individually or communally postulated. Ideas of human nature are historically conditioned, and ideas of God are therefore also historically conditioned. So far as the history of religions is concerned it is undeniable that religion is very close to culture, and God to ethnicity. Thus in every society there are certain treasured symbols of national identity – and they are invariably placed in the sacred realm. At a time of acute crisis, when the national identity is threatened, even the most atheistic societies still turn to religion as they have always done. Now, if we had access to a metaphysical realm and to a universal metaphysical God independent of society, language and history, it would be difficult to understand why the ideas of God that are actually held in human societies should be so highly culture-specific and so fiercely-contested. But, I suggest, the endless contestation of the idea of God reflects conflict between human groups and human individuals as they define their own ideals and identities in apposition and opposition to each other. Gods are always ethnic personifications.

Our first disregarded feature of the idea of God, then, is that contrary to the impression which philosophical theologies seek to create, ideas of God are inevitably culture-specific. I say 'seek to create', because the great philosophical theologies of Western Europe, Eastern Europe, Islam and so forth could hardly be totally unaware of their own provenance in particular literary traditions, vocabularies and cultures, Latin, Greek and Arabic. But although the great writers of the Middle Ages strove mightily to transcend the limits of their own historically-conditioned vocabularies, they could not deliver. Language can never achieve the transcendence of itself that it keeps appearing to promise. In particular, any term in Latin, Greek or Arabic that is predicated by God, whether affirmatively or negatively, must by its use tie God back into the local cultural tradition even as the human writer is professing to break out of it.[7] Thus, if he declares that God is not-p, his statement still depends for its intelligibility upon the contingent human context of p, and so binds God to that milieu. Any God whom language can conjure up can't help but be a local God, tied to that local language, values and world-view. But the great philosophical theologies of the past would not concede the point. Without exception they claimed that the God of whom they spoke was universal and not just local, and they held that their own limitations in speaking of him were likewise universal and metaphysical and not just cultural.

Secondly, God is not seen but heard. The gods of polytheism were primarily visual objects, shining and beautiful Forms. I do not intend the least disrespect to them when I say that their status was very like that of modern media images, and in particular animated cartoon characters. They were identified by a simple fixed iconography and their images were well-established in the culture, widely-diffused, and part of everyone's consciousness. Notice especially that every image of Donald Duck really is Donald Duck himself, while yet there is no single object that you can point to as being uniquely and exclusively the real Donald

Duck. He exists only as an image and as such it is essential that he be infinitely multipliable. Every image of him is as much he as any other. But the images have no referent beyond themselves, and no particular manifestation of Donald Duck is specially privileged.

We observe here the gains and losses of being just an image. The price that must be paid for ubiquity is that in order to be everywhere you must accept the status of a simplified and infinitely-multipliable image. As such, Donald Duck is first and foremost a *visual* image. The voice is very familiar, indeed is universally known and loved, but the visual image is prior and by it Donald Duck is immediately identified. Compared with, say, a signature-tune, a visual image is very much more quick, complete and unmistakable. You can forget or misidentify signature-tunes, but nobody ever forgot Donald Duck. Saints in the Middle Ages (and politicians today in the work of cartoonists) similarly tend to be iconographically fixed with a few standard visual cues.

However, with the God of monotheism it is precisely this entire visual apparatus – the iconography, the cues for identification, the endless multiplication of images and the privileging of vision over sound – which tends to disappear, and usually is prohibited. It seems that God must not become a visually-identifiable individual. Instead God is manifested almost exclusively to the sense of hearing, and in particular as language. And it must be said that the philosophical tradition has never offered any very clear explanation of why it is that God is audio and not video. The usual explanation – in terms of 'idolatry', and images being 'merely creaturely' – is worthless, because an audio God who takes the form of a human-type Voice speaking a human language has thereby seen just as much brought down into the realm of the merely sensuous, finite and human as a video God who is represented in the form of a human body.

So, and thirdly then, God in monotheism is a speaker of language, and the two most obviously-relevant features of audio as distinct from video are that Voice is a far more explicit and powerful medium than vision for conveying prescriptions, commanding, laying down the Law and setting standards, and also that audio is more intimate and searching than video can ever become. To take the latter point first, when we hear, each of us hears for herself. Hearing is more internal. I hear in my ears, whereas what is seen is seen as being out there in the public realm and visible to all. As everyone has noticed, radio and personal stereo seem to get inside one's head, and to be much more inward than video.

Thus the God who is Voice is able to be both more specifically-commanding *and* more inward, both more publicly-authoritative and more in the heart, than the older visual Gods. The shift to audio marks a huge advance in God's power and authority. Insofar as there was a clear changeover from the typically-Hellenic privileging of vision to the typically-Hebraic privileging of voice, we can now suggest what it involved and why it occurred. In the Axial Period, the early Iron Age, we observe the rise of a vigorous and questioning spiritual individualism. Society gradually learns to cope with it by the shift from video to audio. This makes possible the cultural implanting of a powerful inner monitor in each person's head, making social control at once more personalized and more effective. People learn to speak of conscience, calling, vocation, guidance and so on – phrases indicating that authoritative inner voices are now telling them individually how to live.

Scripture suggests that the divine Voice when at its most powerful was heard in two main ways. The first and most highly regarded was the prophetic oracle, especially when it came spontaneously rather than being induced. Unanimously the texts inform us that the Word of the Lord came to the prophet in the form of a private auditory hallucination, unheard by other people.[8] The prophet would then simply repeat it to its appointed addressees, prefixing it by a standard formula such as 'Thus says Yahweh'. The only way in which the addressees could test the authority and authenticity of the oracle was by paying attention to the prophet's manner of life, his established reputation, the outcome of his previous oracles and so on.

The auditory hallucination was, inevitably, solitary. There seems to be no case of two different prophets having been independently charged by God with just the same oracle to deliver. The alternative route by which God might speak could more often and more easily become communal, because ecstasy and trance are highly contagious. In this case, then, the ecstatic individual or group would fall into trance and become the mouthpiece or medium through which God spoke directly to the addressees. Because in such a case the medium is not in normal consciousness, the oracle might be enigmatic, or it might be chaotic. Bands of ecstatic prophets, congregations in glossolalia and teams of shamans may have a great deal too much to say. Skilled interpreters may well be needed to make sense of it all.

Around the fifth century BCE the direct hearing of divine voices was fading away fast in both Greece and Israel. Scriptural religion is based on the presumption that the age of prophecy is over. Nothing must be lost from what has been spoken to us by God so far, and nothing more may be added. The canon is complete, the book of Truth is full. But although from now on the religious authorities – basically, a group of scribes and priestly guardians of true doctrine – are going to be highly suspicious of any self-styled prophet, the whole system still presupposes and depends upon the old divine auditions. Scripture's authority depends upon the belief that there can be such a thing as an authentic divine Voice, which some people really have heard. The Book claims to preserve authentic memories of it and to be an adequate replacement for it. Furthermore, although the leadership certainly does not wish to have any fresh prophets pretending to have heard from God and therefore threatening to modify the existing body of religious truth, we are nevertheless expected to go on finding the idea of a supernatural communication of language into our souls intelligible. It lives on in a wide range of metaphors. Plato's writing on the soul and Jeremiah's writing in the heart[9] introduced a metaphor still not dead, and people speak even yet of the voice of conscience, the call of God and of inspiration. Schizophrenics still hear voices, though today they are less likely to emanate from the objects of traditional belief. As often as not they are beamed into the subject's head by radio from spaceships. Still, the ancient doctrine remains: a god is a Voice that talks straight into your head.

A fourth and very significant feature of the idea of God is that he was described as a continuously uprushing and present-tense power and energy. The long dominance of philosophical theism has always tended to make God into a rather inert, static and timeless Absolute. His intense Now-ness has been converted into 'Eternity', and his raging furious creative activity into eternal foreordination. So philosophy tamed and sterilized God. But in prephilosophical times Spirit was associated with rushing movement such as that of wind and storm and mighty waters. God was a hectic, outpouring productive energy, always Now, always present and active. In Exodus the celebrated and endlessly-discussed Tetragrammaton, the four-lettered name of God, 'I Am', signifies God's self-affirmation, temporal presence and causal and performative power.[10] It is because God is something very like the continual welling-up of life itself that to this day the idioms in which we talk about Life – how it is, how it is treating us and how we feel about it – are so interestingly close to the idioms in which we talk about God. In later theology, after Plato, the removal of God to a timeless abstract heavenly world outside life made it very difficult to see how God could, in even the most extended analogical sense, be described as living. But in archaic times there was not that difficulty. God really *was* Life, pouring out in language.

Finally, the strong emphasis in monotheism upon the Unity – absolute, newly-achieved and therefore all the more vehemently affirmed – of both God and his little image, the human soul, marks God's having become the monarchical principle of Reason, long-termism and the Law. Reality has been organized into a tightly-run pyramid-structure both at the macrocosmic and at the microcosmic levels. God prescribes the structure both of the natural world and of the social world. He differentiates everything, sets all the standards, lays down the Law, and says how things must be. To repeat what has been said earlier, God is a linguistic idealist and an expressivist. More than that, he is a Lord and an ordainer. He does not create merely in the sense of (indicatively) just making the world out of nothing. He commands it to be, he prescribes its structure. He *orders* it in two senses at once, commanding its arrangement. The philosophical tradition oddly forgets the *imperative-performative* (and linguistic) character of the Creator's act.

We have been suggesting that the whole philosophical tradition has either repressed or at any rate neglected these very simple and primal features of the idea of God. It has always striven to locate the divine in a timeless universal intelligible world that is somehow supposed to be independent of particular human societies, their histories and their evolving languages. Christianity, wishing for its own purposes to draw a clear distinction between the unchanging Truth of divine Revelation and all merely human truths, was glad to take over the platonic scheme of thought. But this has made it difficult for us to recognize that all religious and philosophical vocabularies are developed within cultural traditions, and that there always has been and still is a profound link between religion, language and ethnicity.

It has also made it difficult for us to see that the philosophical tradition was from the first founded on certain deceptions and repressions. Plato gave the impression that we are capable of nonlinguistic thought, and that the meanings of words are unchanging, objective intelligible essences, *noēta*. Language starts in one person's mouth and stops in another person's ear. Within the ear the meanings are extracted from the noise-packaging in which they were transmitted, and then pure thought takes over. Pure thought, manipulating pure *noēta*, operates in a realm beyond space and time. Did Plato really think all this? Did he suppose that there was a kind of pre-established harmony between the vocabulary of his Greek, as it was used just in his own time, and the world of eternal Forms, so that, by a stunning coincidence, there was an exact one-to-one correspondence between the range of Intelligible Forms in the noumenal world and the range of words available in the human language here below? We cannot answer this question, because it could not even have been asked before the present century; and the fact that we now cannot help but ask it shows that we have somehow slipped away from Plato and have lost communication with him. For we are now impelled to ask of him questions that *in principle* he (that is, his text) cannot answer.

For us Plato has become encapsulated, his dream of transcendence having been relativized. As it now appears, the entire history of religions knows of no fully universal God of the platonic type, because there is no unchanging universal vocabulary in which to name him and speak of him. (And note that masculine pronoun, for a start.) All gods and accounts of God are tied into the vocabularies of particular peoples and culture-areas. For each of us humans there is bound to be an intimate connection between on the one hand our ideas about God and the sacred realm, and on the other hand the contingent human vocabulary with which our culture has programmed us. Our religion cannot help but be local and human, not absolute.

Now let us put together the various repressed or neglected primal features of the idea of God that we have reviewed. He is an intense uprushing life-energy, profoundly linguistic, world-ordering, an admonitory Voice internal to the self and always temporally present, programmed into us by culture in a highly culture-specific way that gives us our cultural identity ... what is all this adding up to? Evidently talk about God, originally at least, was rooted in a shared experience of a burning sacred energy inside us which manifested itself in the creative and world-ordering power of language. As all scriptures insist, God is not far away. In fact, God is closer to us than we are to ourselves, so close as to be invisible, so close indeed as to be transcendental, for he is the power of language-in-the-unconscious to call life forth into expression and to order the world. God is something like an endlessly self-outpouring Now, a fountain of linguistic meanings that wells up within us and pours out through us on to our world.

Look inside yourself for a moment. Somewhere a bit behind

your eyes and a bit above your soft palate there is going on just now a super-rapid whirring and churning of half-formed and only-partly-articulated words and sentences. A seething primal soup of language; a crucible.[11] You will have noticed the phenomenon when, under pressure, you have been forced to think very fast. Your extra-high level of brain arousal, with the pulse racing at 130-plus, makes you a notch or two more highly conscious than usual, and you can feel the working of your own language-generator. At the opposite extreme, you will also have been able to detect it in operation when you are very relaxed and drifting in the twilit region between sleep and waking. Here too, language is experienced as autonomous, self-proliferating and coming up from below. You do not yourself cause all these images and sentences to run around, and in any case you recognize that the spotlight of consciousness illuminates only a minute fraction of them all. The language-generating area of the brain freewheels very fast all the time, fantasizing, simulating possible courses of events, riffling through vocabulary, trying out part-sentences and generating hypotheses. Compared with the conscious self it is both extremely quick and also somewhat irresponsible. It plays with language – that is, with the signifier, with the contingent marks and sounds that words are – in somewhat the way that the setters of crossword-puzzles do. It loves puns, associations, metaphors and *double-entendre*. It enjoys not just onomatopoiea but even more the graphic equivalent of onomatopoiea, for which our language has no word. Thus the English-speaking unconscious delights in the world 'goggles' and instinctively associates it with perfectly circular lenses, because the 'gog' of goggles, when written carelessly in ordinary longhand, actually *looks* rather like a pair of spectacles. Again, the first person singular pronoun 'I' felicitously looks like a unit, a number one and a standing person, and sounds like an 'eye', a subject with a point of view. For a third and final example, the zero and capital O looks like the shape we make with our lips in order to pronounce it, 'eau', and evokes a range of related words also with 'o's in them, which suggests emptiness – no, nothing, hole, void, orifice. Very inter-

estingly, the absurdity, the materiality and the accidental felicities
of language, which so scandalize rationalism, are a matter of
delight to the Unconscious. It loves the play of the signifier, and
it has to be disorderly in order to generate innovations.

When Freud's work was first received in the English-speaking
world there was a tendency to read him in terms of Darwin and
of *Dr Jekyll and Mr Hyde*. The Unconscious was the beast beneath
the skin, it was a leftover from our evolutionary history, it was
a cluster of strong animal impulses such as gentlemen were supposed to keep under control and ladies entirely lacked. However
there is also in Freud – in the book on jokes, for example – what
one might call a Jewish Unconscious, super-verbal, a lover of
symbols, puns, deceptions, word-play, masks, disguises, tall
stories, evasions and fanciful interpretations. More recently, since
Lacan and post-structuralism, it has become easier to recognize
that the Unconscious is cultural rather than natural, that it is
linguistic, that it is prodigiously creative and that it encompasses a
vast range, from mediating to us society's moral and religious
norms, through spontaneously generating myths, metaphors and
hypotheses, to a delight in mischief and ribaldry.

All this whirling logorrhea has a straightforward function: it
keeps close to hand a very large range of resources for structuring,
valuing and interpreting experience. The quicker it all runs, the
shorter our reaction time. With the help of that fizzing dynamo
of meanings we are constantly scanning, experimenting with
recollections, scenarios, interpretations and theories. When the
machinery throws up a scrap of narrative, a word, an image, a
pattern that fits, that switches us on, that engages us, that makes
libido flow – then, at that instant, a little ripple of feeling in us gets
coded as a meaning and enters consciousness as a datum of
experience. We are alive, and tuned in.[12]

It is the ceaseless hectic upsurge of language in the Unconscious
that powers our life. We human beings live in language. We can
only get to the world through language. The language-generator
supplies the interpretative resources that keep us locked on to the
world, that keep libido switched on and that we use to structure

and interpret the world. I can experience *only* what I've got words for. Words bring us to life and make our world. So the God of speech is postulated as the source of (or is just identified with) this flow of meaning both in society generally and in the individual.

The connection between God and the Unconscious was made, of course, both by Jung and by William James. Before them, it was a common theme of the Romantics. The process by which an artist consults the Unconscious or waits for the right idea or image to come is very similar to the way a religious person waits upon God in prayer. After German Idealism had made God transcendental and inward, so that he was experienced as a Power that comes into expression through us rather than as a Being who stands over against us, artistic inspiration and divine inspiration became indistinguishable. As when we put a shell to our ear we seem to hear the distant sound of the sea, so under certain conditions we may seem to hear the language-dynamo in us. It is the prodigiously-rich background from which we select out our thin, disciplined and linear sentences; and in this relation between the consciously-produced linear sentence and the vast background of linguistic excess from which it has been extracted we may trace the origin of the distinction between the self and God, the finite and the infinite.

In glossolalia and delirium the language-dynamo breaks the surface. Something of its raging, excessive energy is directly heard because the narrowing and selecting activity of ordinary consciousness has been suspended. The resulting ecstasy or frenzy was always regarded as a supernaturally-inspired state. But what of the other case of divinely-inspired speech, the prophetic oracle? Jung must be right: it is possible for some part of the language-machine to take on a distinct personality. The unconscious is social; it has religious and ethical imperatives written into it, and if they are disregarded it becomes fretful. Where the local culture provides appropriate forms, it is not surprising that religious imperatives should be able to assume an accusing Voice of their own, telling me that I fall short of their requirements, or constraining me to act as their mouthpiece in attacking an hypocritical society that pays them only lipservice. Jeremiah testifies that the pent-up Voice inside him rocked his body with the violence of its demand for expression.[13]

Along these lines, then, religious beliefs may be seen as words about words – an entirely intelligible way of speaking about what language is, how it arises in us and how it empowers us and orders our world. We can see why belief in God feels so completely natural to people, and why they think of God as being so close, so powerful, so articulate, and as creating all things by the word of his mouth. Just what it is to think, the very way in which sentences come to birth in us, seems to confirm belief in God. Everyone who has waited for the right word to come, everyone who has had a bright idea, has already an experiential context into which to fit talk of divine grace and inspiration. Everyone who has felt pangs of conscience knows how readily they become an accusing and reproachful Voice. Furthermore, since very much the same cultural and linguistic resources are programmed into each individual member of a language-group, and since our meanings, our idioms and our valuations are kept in close alignment by our daily linguistic exchanges, God-talk is both intimately applicable to each individual and publicly meaningful for everyone. Language has no difficulty in being both the most subjectively-penetrating and the most objectively-real thing there is.

A curious and interesting problem remains, though. The language-dynamo in the Unconscious is very often far more mischievous, bubbling, ribald, anarchic and disorderly than the later God of Writing is supposed to be. Why is this? Why did God cool down so much?

In preliterate and early literate times the Sacred was very often experienced as non-rational, mischievous and disorderly. People didn't seem to worry about it. Life's like that. There were Gods of Fortune and Gods of Wine. Even the God of Israel was, as everyone knows, perfectly capable of sending evil, tempting people and being outrageous and difficult. So God was clearly recognized as having a dark, irrational and wayward side to him, like language and like us.

Early Christianity, you may think, was different – puritanical, keen on self-control and emphasizing the consistency of God's character. Yet the early church knew the divine delirium of glossolalia from the day of Pentecost onwards, and, oddly, even Paul does not altogether prohibit such fits of insanity and linguistic excess outright, as being incompatible with the controlled rationality of God's Word.[14] But then, at that early stage Christianity was in effect still prescriptural. It had not yet fully transferred its allegiance to the new God of Writing.

Appendix

For some years I have put forward views about language that stand broadly in the tradition that runs from Nietzsche and Freud to Lacan and post-structuralism. However, in the English-speaking world the dominant group at present are those people who are trying to build theories in the region between neuro-science and cognitive science. The most-discussed work is that of D. E. Rumelhart and J. L. McClelland (see the two volumes of *Parallel Distributed Processing: Explorations in the Microstructure of Cognition*, MT Press 1986: Vol. 1, ed. G. E. Hinton, McClelland and Rumelhart; Vol. 2, ed. McClelland, Rumelhart and the PDP Research Group.)

From our point of view there are two plusses in recent scientific work on language: it tends to dissolve the received distinction between language comprehension and language generation, which not long ago were assigned to quite different areas of the brain, and it has shown how seemingly rule-following linguistic behaviours can be built up without any need to postulate either Chomskyan innate rules or any deliberate formulation of rules.

So far so good: but of course my emotivist view of language, and my semi-biological picture of rational sense as what gets

selected out by cultural training from a rich unconscious background of divine nonsense, are at the opposite pole from the
highly scientized computer modelling now generally favoured.

Roughly, if my emotivism is right, a computer will never really
be able to *take part* in a conversation. Without the play of feeling
and nonsense, conversing with a computer is never going to be
more than a special case of operating a machine. Whereas if the
PDP approach is right, then it may as easily be used to teach a
computer to speak, as a human being. In principle, the two cases
are on the same level.

From my point of view the PDP-model approach makes the
old mistake of prioritizing indicative fact-stating sentences, as if
all the other uses of language were secondary or less important.
Whereas I want to say that the rhetoric comes first: until you
have some capacity to tell what sort of game is being played,
you cannot join in. However good you are at generating
grammatically-correct sentences, you can contribute nothing
apposite unless you know, for example, whether the last thing
said was intended seriously. This calls for a kind of emotional
attunement that is beyond the reach of a machine.

A paradox: in the understanding of language, rhetoric is
logically prior to logic. Another paradox: if you are built to play
only one language game, then you will not be able to play even
that one correctly. You will not be able to identify it, because you
know nothing of the alternatives *vis-à-vis* which it is defined.

3. *The God of writing*

The previous section was secretly toubled by a paradox: the God
of speech, that is, the God of late pre-scriptural religion based on
spontaneous eruptions of the divine Voice in the human psyche,
is inevitably known of only through writing. And for most of its
history writing has been complaining about its own second or
third rate status. It has regarded itself as but a poor substitute for
speech, which in turn is merely an exterior clothing of thoughts.
In addition, although forceful speech is action, writing is mere

recollection. Writing is Silver-Age. It is secondary, only a memorandum. Even to the present day many or most writers are nostalgic conservatives who look back to an earlier generation when the culture was allegedly in better shape than it is now. Writing is always deferring to and yearning for a lost presence and immediacy. Some degree of alienation or absence is its precondition. So how do we know that the God of speech is not just another literary fantasy? Don't almost all writings seem to suggest that in an earlier generation people were closer to God than they are now? The very nature of writing is such as to generate such a belief. Writing is reliving in solitary reverie: its posture is one of looking back to a lost paradise or a heroic age.[15]

This 'literary' and nostalgic type of writing is though a fairly late development. The very earliest writing was simpler and more functional. It was a record, an aide-memoire or a script for performance, rather than an independent work of art to be perused silently for one's own pleasure and profit. Reading meant reading aloud, so that the written text had something of the status of a musical score, being not itself the music but merely a set of instructions for producing the music. Jeremiah saw his writings as being like pre-electric gramophone records: he dictated the words to his scribe who wrote them down on a scroll, which the scribe then took to the addressee and read aloud to him.[16] The purpose of writing it all down was to ensure accurate sound reproduction. This was indeed the normal method of delivering a letter: the written text of the letter was carried by the messenger, not to be handed over to the addressee, but as a production-script used by him to prompt himself as he recited his message. Is that not why we still have ambassadors even to this day? Really important messages must be delivered orally by a fully-briefed and accredited representative, who is treated as being in effect the king whose mouthpiece he is.

Writing first began, then, as a minimal notation for recording transactions, payments, stocks, dates and the like. It soon became a way of recording laws, annals, ritual instructions, letters, the calendar, and even myths for recitation at festivals. In due course it developed into a way of evoking a lost Golden Age when the Gods and human beings were close to each other. But in all these uses writing is a secondary reminder. The graphic sign remains as distinct from the thing signified as the knot in my handkerchief is from the task of buying a birthday present of which it reminds me. Furthermore, a written sign by its nature is liable to live on, distinct from its writer and the original occasion of writing, until it eventually becomes quite indecipherable. Writing lives while it can re-mind the reader of something other than itself.

Yet if the written sign is thus seen as something weak, secondary, dissociated, and lacking in any intrinsic potency, we may well ask how in that case a written text could ever have come to be 'the Word of God'? Surely the traditional theories and functions of writing that we have briefly reviewed make it impossible to see how mere writing could ever be able to re-present or communicate to us the full presence and power of God?

It was in the hope of overcoming these perceived limitations of writing that a strengthened form of the prophet Jeremiah's gramophone-record theory was revived in the West after the invention of printing. In the sixteenth century the churches, Catholic and Protestant alike, defined the canon of scripture and developed very 'literalistic' divine-dictation theories of biblical inspiration. The idea was that scholarship or church authority – or a judicious admixture of both – would fix the correct text of Holy Writ, and printing would then reproduce it in large quantities. In this way the relationship between God, the scriptural writer, the text and each individual modern reader would parallel the relationship between Jeremiah, his secretary Baruch, the scroll of written-down prophecies and King Jehoiakim, long ago. Faithful reproduction was guaranteed. The modern reader would hear the exact words God had uttered, without any distortion; and perhaps, too, God's Spirit in my heart would ensure that I correctly grasped what God had meant by uttering just these words.

Yes, but the biggest difficulty still remains. Jeremiah's oracles were repeated to the king in person on the same day. The point of writing them down had been to prompt Baruch, and also to symbolize the irrevocability of the message. The king, enraged, cut up the scroll and burnt it on the spot, but Jeremiah replied by dictating a fresh scroll 'with many similar words'.[17] Jehoiakim was not going to get away with it. The oracles of the God of speech were thus highly topical and individually-addressed. When the prophet or his representative arrived at the door, you might not look forward to the interview, but there was little danger of boredom. What the prophet had to say was addressed to you personally and was very much *a propos*. 'Have you found me, O my enemy?', says the unfortunate Ahab. 'I have', replies Elijah grimly,[18] and proceeds to give the king an earful such as would no longer be possible after the rise of scriptural religion, when the prophet has been replaced by a mere lesson-reader and the oracle by a standard cycle of readings. Religious truth in the age of writing is something that was delivered complete long ago and is already known to everyone. A Bible is a standard oracle, for millions, for millennia. God lacks his old overwhelming power and immediacy of address to the individual in the Now: like truth, God has become timeless and standardized. When the Rule of Faith becomes in perpetuity just a mass-produced Book, God suffers a certain depersonalization. Is this progress? And how strange it is that in the sixteenth century the Protestant Reformers and the Council of Trent should have toiled away with their dictation-theories and other devices to give scripture infallible authority as the Word of God addressed personally to us, while yet scripture itself perversely persists in undermining itself by recalling so eloquently a lost immediacy that it can never hope to replace.

Hence the pessimism of Protestants. The more highly you rate the authority of the Bible, the more you must be convinced by it of the infinite inferiority of the scriptural phase of religion to the first-hand experience that preceded it and that will follow it. The Protestant lives by very elaborate written guarantees about what has happened in the past and what we may hope for in the future; but because nothing may imperil or question the certainty of those guarantees, the Protestant's present-day worship, belief, experience and practice must be very low-key and confined strictly within scriptural limits. There can be no interesting innovation, only active obedience and patient waiting. When the last apostolic writer laid down his pen the Book was finished and religion was frozen until the return of Christ. Apostolic inspiration, prophecy, miracles and the like all ceased. From now on God's relationship to humankind was supposed to be mediated through the 'Paper Pope' and its various interpreters. Yet, ironically, the very preachers and theologians who taught the slogan *sola scriptura* (by scripture alone, because scripture only contains all things necessary to salvation) themselves still made a living out of controlling the way it was interpreted. Evidently no text, not even scripture, can really stand alone. It promptly blends into, or vanishes into, an endless interpretative conversation about itself. And because scripture thus turned out to be secondary like all other writing, the Protestant God disappeared into it. By a development whose oddity we too seldom notice, the very word 'divinity' had already during the later Middle Ages come to mean just a branch of literary study, sacred learning. God is letters.

There is an elegant illustration of all this in the narrative which describes the institution of scriptural religion in Israel. The events took place in Jerusalem in the seventh month, probably of the year 397 BCE. The restoration of Jewish life after the Babylonian exile had been laborious and slow, but the Persian kings had permitted some resettlement. An encircling city wall and a modest temple had been built, but the voice of prophecy was silent and religious institutions were weak. Many of the elite of the Jewish people still lived in Babylon. There they had apparently codified their religion, making it into a book. Probably many books, but the one in question here was called the book of the law of Moses. It was an early recension of the Jewish Torah.

In Nehemiah 8, a Persian court official entitled 'Ezra the priest, the script of the law of the God of heaven' arrives in Jerusalem with this 'book of the law of Moses'. Such a book is not only a compilation of traditions from the past, but also a programme for reform and a manifesto for the future. The people gather in the square by the Water Gate. Standing in a wooden pulpit, Ezra reads aloud from the holy book all morning. Alas, from its very first day in use scripture was already a little archaic, read out in classical Hebrew to a people who were going over to Aramaic, and describing traditions and rituals that had become unfamiliar to them. A whole team of interpreters was needed to give a running paraphrase and commentary as Ezra read.

The people are deeply moved to hear about their own half-forgotten ancestral traditions, and straightaway begin the observance of the Feast of Ingathering or Tabernacles in the manner laid down in the book. During it they gather daily for further readings from the book. In fact they are now constituted, in a way they had never been before, as the People of the Book. So at least an evidently idealized narrative suggests.

This is scriptural religion, religion codified, written down, systematized, rounded off and closed. From this day on people will increasingly tend to think of religious truth as something given, routinized and unalterable. It no longer bursts out unpredictably in the way it once did. Nor does God. God and his Word to human beings have lost their old excessiveness and have become rationalized. The professionals have taken over. So far as the common people of Jerusalem are concerned, religion has become something drawn up for them and explained to them by a remote scholarly class who serve a great Emperor in a distant city. The old popular charismatic figures have been replaced by the new functionaries of literate civilization, the Masters of Sacred Letters: the scribe, the canonist, the preacher, the theologian, the teacher, the writer, the professor.

And yet it is scripture that tells us what a letdown scripture is!

We are suggesting, then, that the whole history of religious thought in the West has been clouded by certain doctrines about, and a certain hierarchizing of, speech and writing. The highest value was always ascribed to face-to-face encounter, unmediated presence – in a word, speech. In the early church the 'living voice' of the oral tradition was for centuries prized more highly than the written word, and Roman Catholics still believe in an oral, un-written tradition of religious truth.[19] It was very difficult to admit that the religion of Christians too is only – and inescapably – a religion of the letter, exactly like Judaism.

However, following the modern metaphysics of writing, I want to argue that the old habit of prioritizing speech and down-grading writing was a mistake. Speech, too, is nothing but a stringing together of publicly-conventionalized signs, and nothing whatever guarantees that speech is less likely than writing to be ambiguous or misunderstood. Anyone who has lectured to a large audience knows that as many lectures are heard as people are present. And similarly, suppose that God really does speak to me: there is no way I can 'hear' him except in the form of English sentences resounding in my head. Those English sentences will be just as much open to questions concerning their meaning and interpretation as are sentences in a written text. There is an addi-tional difficulty in that in such a case I wouldn't know how to tell whether the words I was hearing were 'mere' subjectively-produced hallucinations, or 'genuine' auditions from God; but that is an independent question and not my present concern. Let us by-pass that issue and grant that I really am receiving genuine supernatural auditions: still, they will have to be in English sen-tences, and I am saying that not even God can create in such a case the pure face-to-face unmistakable immediacy of which people have dreamt. For us human beings who dwell in language and are made of language there is no understanding except *via* words, that is, *via* general signs. As philosophy always acknow-ledged, human understanding is discursive and not immediate. There is no immediacy in language, for general signs strung to-gether in syntagmatic chains will always be open to interpretation.

Briefly, the case for this last point is that a sign's meaning can only be spelled out by differentiating the way it is used from the way its closest neighbours are used. But those neighbours then have to be explained in the same way, and so on for ever. Further-more, all linguistic usages are in slow change. And many or most signs have many different uses. Even if we know just which one applies in a particular case, the others cannot help but be vaguely invoked as well. In addition, there is often room for doubt about the rhetorical situation. 'Was irony intended there? What game is being played?' For these and other reasons meaning in a natural language is always a little cloudy and disputable. It can never be made completely specific, beyond any doubt or question. Nor should we regret this. Since we live entirely within mediacy, secondariness or discursiveness – that is, within language – for us ambiguity and perpetual movement are the very stuff of life itself. Dreams of absolute and intuitive knowledge in a world without doubt or ambiguity should be opposed. They are futile and empty. They serve only to devalue life by making people feel that they are exiled from a better place elsewhere. There is nothing wrong with a little vagueness and ambiguity. It is a condition of life, because historical change cannot take place unless the meanings and valuations associated with words can be shifted a little. Meanings have to be movable, just as libido has to be displaceable.

It now seems that the myth of the primacy of speech developed by way of explaining, deflecting attention away from, and consoling us for the supposed unsatisfactoriness of scriptural religion. For twenty-four centuries God has been in writing, embodied in a group of signs, idioms, texts. At first sight scripture seems a strangely miscellaneous collection of materials, and a large professional class, the Masters of Sacred Letters, has existed to guard these writings, to prove that they have one clear fixed meaning, to keep on reminding us of it, and to keep firm control of it. But unfortunately this rationale for the existence of the Masters of Letters is self-subverting. If God is the master of meaning and the author of scripture, and has spoken his one final Word to humankind, surely he should have been able to make himself plain to us? Does he really need the assistance of a squabbling army of interpreters? Their very existence, their efforts to make God's meaning plain, and their use of coercive methods to protect what they currently claim to be his plain meaning, all undermines their claim that God has successfully made himself plain. We begin to have horrid doubts. Perhaps God himself is nothing but a bunch of signs manipulated to their own advantage by the clerk/clerics? As a defence against this fearsome possibility, scripture itself teaches the myth of the primacy of speech and bears witness to a God of speech, who once, by speaking directly into the individual's soul, cut out the clerkly interpreter and thereby assured all later generations of his own reality. Religious certainty is possible because, so we are told, it once existed.

But the God of speech is mythical. That is to say, there is no way in which God could so speak to me that there could be no doubt, either about who is speaking to me, or about what he means to tell me. How can I be sure that I am not hearing voices, like poor Evelyn Waugh's 'Gilbert Pinfold', and how can I be sure exactly what the words mean? So the God of speech is mythical, or, to be more exact, the notion that speech is qualitatively superior to writing and can be misunderstanding-proofed is mythical. The history of religions indeed reminds us that oracles and tongues also very often need interpreters. So do dreams and visions. Which all goes to show that the limitations of the God of writing apply also to other modes of God's self-communication to human beings.

All theologies, up to Bonhoeffer at least, supposed that God could communicate himself to us human beings, and could yield himself up into the hands of men while yet remaining not less than himself. God in *paradosis* (= traditio) would still be God; the Word of God proceeding forth would still be at his Father's side. But we can no longer see how this could be so. For God is expression, God revealing himself to human beings, is God going out into language. And this is death for God, as it is for all of us, for it requires God to abandon his absoluteness and selfsameness and suffer dispersal into the endlessness of interpretation. He has to go into the ambiguity and secondariness of writing, and like any other speaker of a human tongue he must become in the end nothing but the many different things that others make of him.[20]

Along these lines we can see the kenotic theories of nineteenth-century theologians as interestingly anticipating what can now be said more precisely about the price of God's going into language.

The modern metaphysics of writing has thus had an intricate threefold effect on scriptural religion.

In the first place it has put an end to the idea that some person or institution might have the power and the authority to find and impose the Old True Meaning of Scripture. There is no such thing: scripture is plural. Like any other text, it will mean different things at different times and places and when read from different angles. So we must give up the idea that somebody knows what scripture *really* means.

Secondly, though, we should also be wary of that curious cluster of ideas that led scripture first to stress its own imperfection and secondariness as writing, and then to appeal for its own legitimation to a previous 'God of speech' of which it is itself the only record. In effect, scripture said: 'Though I am admittedly only writing, I am also the appointed and privileged witness to a pure and immediate presence of God in the oracles of the prophets and in the Person of the Incarnate Word of God, Jesus Christ.' This will not do, because the end of the myth of the primacy and superiority of speech means that there isn't anything any longer vis-à-vis which scripture can represent itself as being inferior. Scripture cannot appeal to something outside itself that is religiously superior to itself. There are, for example, no mystical wordless ecstasies that are better than writing. So thirdly, the God of speech, immediately and unmistakably sounding in our heads and giving us guidance, now looks more like a nostalgic myth set up as the correlate of scripture's self-disparagement.

When we become aware of language and accept that it just is what it is, then a number of myths are dispelled. We see that religion's written character, and its openness therefore to endless reinterpretation, is not something to be regretted or resisted but simply something to be used.

4. *The God of language*

The God of writing, as we have seen, is a very complex formation. He is assembled out of writing's insistence on its own imperfection, its retrospective appeal for legitimation to a past immediacy of divine presence of which it is in effect the only record, the use of religious power to control its correct interpretation, and the promise to the patient and vigilant believer that immediacy will be restored in the future. There are four strands here, then: provisionality, a past golden age, authority and a future hope. All of them are needed to make the system work.

The resulting era of writing-based civilization is the historical period, during which human life is lived within certain great disciplinary institutions. The most important of these bodies is the religious society of the people of the Book (the church, the synagogue, Islam . . .) followed by the state, the academy and so on. Within these very powerful organizations human life is lived under rule, a rule made tolerable by being represented as a time of preparation. We are told that the age of God's immediate presence and activity among us is past. It came to an end with the writing of the Book, which is a souvenir of its closure. But scripture also promises the arrival of a new age of perfection in the future. It is called the Last Day, or the Parousia. At first it was expected to come very shortly, but it has been deferred and deferred. History is the extended time of waiting opened up by this repeated postponement of the Parousia. During it no very substantial religious change may take place. The canon is closed. However, we can by various practices express the ardour of our expectation. The most general and important of these endeavours is the task of building up and strengthening the religious institution itself. We need to guard the text and the Truth committed to us. Religious professionals must collaborate in determining, propagating and enforcing the correct interpretation of Revealed Truth, pretty much as the state and its officers interpret, elaborate and extend the sway of the law. The object is, by building up and strengthening the institution, to make the faithful ever more precisionist in their obedience and their observances.

It is as if the institution says to itself, 'We have got all human beings well and truly domesticated by now, *but they are still not nearly domesticated enough!*' So the discipline is elaborated further and further, as though its intensification were an end in itself, while yet the public are simultaneously being assured that the entire system is merely an interim arrangement. Soon the church will wither away, soon the Kingdom of God will come. Meanwhile, as the centuries slip by our lives must apparently become more-and-more-minutely regulated, and all ostensibly for the sake of a future state of perfect *liberty!* Such is the basic contradiction of organized religion: it makes itself an end in itself and becomes ever more bureaucratic, while simultaneously declaring itself to be merely transitional.

This brief analysis suggests connections between a wide range of modern intellectual events. They are all in one way and another signs of the breakup of the cultural formation that we have called 'the God of writing'. The traditional prioritization of speech over writing was based on the claim that speech could escape the secondariness and ambiguity of writing. The speaker could completely control the meaning of his speech. God could therefore go out into utterance and still in his self-expression be completely himself, without suffering any dispersal or dissemination. An immediate Presence of God to humankind was thus possible, so that there really could have been a past Golden Age and there could be a future time of perfection. The superiority of speech was the guarantee of the possibility of a perfect world. Scripture bore witness to the superiority of speech, and hence to the perfect world of Paradise lost and to be restored. But if speech is no better than writing, and if the attempt to find and fix permanently the one true and original meaning of a text must fail, then there cannot be a world that is *both* based on language (as any human world must be) *and* free from ambiguity, disagreement and discord. In which case the belief in a past golden age, the hope of a future one, the supposedly provisional character of the present regime, and the justification for strict interpretative discipline during it all, crumble at once. We suddenly understand how ironical it was that throughout the epoch of sacred literate civilizations writing got its authority from its own self-disparagement. It made itself the necessary bridge between a lost age of immediacy before it and a regained age of immediacy after it. So writing had vast authority so long as it was inferior relative to past and future perfection. But when we began to think that there is nothing wrong with writing because there is nothing superior to it, then it *lost* its old authority, because it ceased to be able to bear authoritative witness to something greater than itself. A certain historicist mythology also ran into difficulties, and people began to talk about the failure of the great 'legitimating narratives', and the end therefore of 'history', in the sense of a progressive movement towards a future consummation of the world which will justify all our present labours and disciplines. There really are very close connections between the 1960s metaphysics of writing and the rise of various sorts of post-historical politics, neo-anarchist and environmentalist. Both groups are trying to go beyond the era of marching-under-discipline towards a future perfection. The anarchist asks why we are still putting up with the rule-book, and the environmentalist calls for a steady-state politics. Both want to live in and for the present.

What of post-historical religion? We use the term 'the God of language' for a time no longer dominated by the priority of speech or the speech-writing distinction. Unable now to look either to the past for legitimation or to the future for justification, we are forced to find and affirm the meaning of our life in the here and now. Since the human condition will never be qualitatively better than it is now, whatever can be done about it has got to be done now.

However, it must be insisted at once that this does not imply any mystical regaining of Presence in the present moment. On the contrary, there is no mastery of the presence of the present moment. We always arrive a little too late, just as self-consciousness always gets there too late. And there can be no going back on the realization that self-expression is death to the speaker, whether the speaker be the Self or God. I am my life, I am my communicative expression; but as I go out into language I lose my self-identity and become nothing but the many different things that people make of me. Like God, we are nothing unless we give ourselves. Our destiny is to give ourselves by going out into communication, but in so giving ourselves we lose control of ourselves. That self-giving is religion, is love, is God and is death. So the God of language is a dying god who continually pours himself out into communication, not minding what people make of him. The God of Christians is a languagey version of Osiris; he reigns in death.

This latest stage of development of the idea of God marks something of a break. The God of speech, whether illusory or not, was the Voice of a namable and personal Spirit. He or she could actually be heard, speaking through the lips of an oracle, a prophetess, or a shaman, resounding in some holy place or simply hallucinated in one's head. At any rate, the testimony is unanimous that authoritative guiding Voices really were heard. They ceased; but the notion of a god as a language-user, and as a real personal being, has lingered on.

The God of writing is surprisingly different. Epiphanies and auditions of Christ, Mary, angels and other figures are frequent. But in Christianity and the other major scriptural traditions direct epiphanies and auditions of God-just-as-God are very rare, and have always been so. The lingering metaphoric of divine voice, word and speech creates an impression that more is being heard from God than is in fact the case. In reality, God has long been completely hidden in writing, and hidden behind the conditions of human existence that he has imposed. He is no longer seen or heard. His proper name has fallen into disuse. In Christianity, he never even had one. He is now only an inferred entity. One tradition maintains that a valid argument for his existence can still be constructed from purely secular or worldly premises. This makes God, in principle, a publicly knowable inferred entity. Others maintain that God can be known only from within religion – only, that is, as the Author of his Revelation, the Father of Jesus Christ and the giver of Grace. This is the non-realism of the Reformed tradition, which makes God an entity that can be inferred only on the basis of faith. The Catholic God is in principle a public object, in a way in which the Protestant God is not. This disagreement between the metaphysical religion of the Catholic tradition and the fideistic religion of the Reformed tradition is certainly important, but it is less important than the point upon which they are in tacit agreement: under the present dispensation God is veiled.

God is hidden behind the basic conditions of human existence, and hidden in Writing. And this veiling of God in the heyday of Writing had a curious consequence. It allowed the self to become like a little god, a self-consciousness certain of itself by virtue of the clarity and distinctness with which it perceived itself. The self was seen as being centred in itself and master of itself. We see the Sun five minutes late, but in self-consciousness there was thought to be no such time-lag. In the philosophy of subjectivity the self is self-founded, self-same and in perfect coincidence with itself. It is indeed a little god.

As everyone knows, these doctrines were stated with great clarity by Descartes. From this, however, people too easily go on to suggest that it was he who originated them, that they are atheistic in tendency, and that in Rousseau and the German Idealists the modern philosophy of subjectivity became more and more inflated until eventually it exploded. But this story overlooks Descartes' traditionalism. He was a student of Augustine and Aquinas, and his philosophy of subjectivity has deep roots in the Western tradition. From the beginning, philosophy had always been rationalistic and had always taught a kind of *supernaturalism of consciousness*, as if the self were a spirit that could function independently of the body, language and culture. In the entire Plato-to-Kant era there is surprisingly little recognition of how flimsy and partial our consciousness is, how imperfect and how secondary. Recognition of the secondariness of consciousness actually begins in Western thought in the very period when, according to the conventional story, the human self was becoming most over-inflated. That consciousness follows and depends upon the common language had scarcely been said clearly before Herder and Hegel said it, and that consciousness follows and depends upon biological processes and drives of which it is the frail and shallow epiphenomenon was scarcely said clearly before

Schopenhauer,[21] who took a great and justifiable pride in his own originality upon this very point.

I am suggesting that an over-inflated conception of the self as a more-or-less free-standing and self-mastering spiritual subject is by no means a modern aberration. It did not begin with Descartes. Spiritual individualism can be traced back into classical antiquity, and was always a possible corollary of the theological tradition. For God was seen as a self-founding Creator-Subject who generates both reality and his own knowledge of it, and the human self was regarded as having been made by God in his own image. The self was from the first a little counterpart of God. Furthermore, during the whole era of 'the God of writing' God had veiled himself, leaving the human subject to be his vice-gerent. In God's absence, the human self expanded. Given this background, it is hardly surprising that the rise of the modern state and early-modern science and technology should have been accompanied by a near divinization of the self. It was an event that had long been waiting to happen.

With the Romantic movement came a much-needed corrective, the return of the self into nature and into history. The thinking subject sinks down and becomes immersed in the body, in language, in culture and in the historical process. Very soon the consciousness of the individual subject begins to seem something secondary. For example, it takes different forms in different historical epochs. Evidently, then, our subjective consciousness is not something supernatural and extra-historical. On the contrary, it is a variable cultural product.

It took a long time, and the work of many thinkers (including Marx, Nietzsche, Freud and Derrida) to complete the de-centring of consciousness. But after we have accepted the idea that our own subjective consciousness is not a pure self-present spirit but something merely secondary, derived and contingent, a new religious possibility appears. We may see religion as a way in which the conscious self relates itself to the upsurging flow of language-and-life-energy that is continuously producing and dispersing it. A spirituality becomes then a religious stance by which we, so-to-say, cope with our own ephemerality.

On this reading God-talk has a purely empirical meaning. Hence our talk of a break. The God of speech was experienced as a personal being, who spoke with an audible voice. The God of writing was a transcendent inferred entity. The God of language is a symbol of where words come from. He is a symbol for the continuously upsurging creative movement of language itself, in which we live and move and have our being. Everything gets compressed into the moment and into spirituality. The flow of the common language through us structures the world, by our own contribution to language we do our little bit to change the world, and by passing out into language ourselves we die into the world. So language all the time is making and unmaking us, but we can make a personal contribution to it. We can disturb language a little as it flows through us. Thus the decentred consciousness, just in its relation to its own life, finds a new way of being religious.

Everything depends upon our being so trained that we get our own relationship to life just right. The point of religious writing is to analyse that relationship, and show how its three principal elements fit together.

The first element is *affirmation*. One should say Yes to life. But we do not in the pagan manner attempt to say Yes just to the natural world, for the supposed natural world is not a fixed quantity. Our theory of it, through which we apprehend it, is changing and developing all the time. It changes, and our activities are changing it. Green fundamentalism is thus a delusion. We do not know of any objective and unchanging natural order out there, such as we might conserve, or fit into or conform ourselves to. What we affirm and say 'Yes' to is not a state of affairs but a process – what people call 'life'. 'Life' is the continuous production of culture as a moving system of signs, and of nature within culture. So to say 'Yes' to life is to say 'Yes' to a creative and productive activity whose source is entirely mysterious to us, but which generates language and culture, and is all the time producing our vision of the world, our feelings and our valuations.

We are not speaking of any energy or force such as might figure in a scientific theory. We are speaking of something that comes before science and makes it possible, namely the generation of a highly-differentiated cultural world of meanings, with feelings and valuations annexed to different zones. Through this creative activity there comes into being all the time a life-world that is structured, significant and interesting, within which we can live and act. Life is all the time giving us a world.

So on our account what used to be called 'believing the doctrine of Creation' takes the form of saying Yes to life, which means receiving as a continually-renewed gift the life-world and our own capacity to live a life within it. Whereas the old Cartesian sort of consciousness used to seem completely on top of things, master of itself, its meanings and its world and monarch of all it surveyed, the newer de-centred sort of consciousness knows that it is only secondary and has every reason to be grateful to life. Only since we are always already within language and culture, of which we are the products, and since we can never get right outside them, we cannot by a transcendental analysis work our way back behind language to discover what is its source.[22] Whatever neologisms we coin in our attempt to investigate a world anterior to language must themselves at once become part of the language. So while the modern discovery of culture and language, and of the secondariness of subjective consciousness, calls for the return of a religious attitude to life, it also compels that religion to be more agnostic and more autonomous than the religion of earlier periods.

So much of the first strand or element of our relation to life, that which we called affirmation. We accept, rejoice in and go along with life's gift of itself and of a life-world to us. We are not talking about a world of atoms and molecules. We are not talking about science at all. We are talking about the givenness of life and of a life-world, a world of meanings and values, that is, a world of *language*, within which intelligible and value-realizing action is possible. Science can get going only *after* all this is in place. The very large and slightly absurd object that physicists call the Universe can only be produced if the life-world is already first given.

The second element of our relation to life I shall call *transformation*. By this I mean that we do not simply accept and affirm the life-world just as it presents itself. In religion, ethics and politics we are also able to act. We put a bit of personal spin upon the language that flows through us, and so make a small contribution to changing language, changing valuations and thereby changing the world. But life itself is an ever-changing thing, and it has also given to us, along with language, a measure of power to change things. So our striving to change the world is itself a part of the whole process of world-making. In theological language, there is not the contradiction that there may seem to be between the ideas of creation and redemption. It can seem at first glance that the creation-theme, which expresses satisfaction with the world as it is, contradicts the redemption-theme, which is dissatisfied and sets out to make a better world. But if the making of the world is a continuous process, and if our capacity to bend language a little and so change things is given as part of the process of world-making, then the redemption of the world may be seen as part of the creation of the world.

Metaphorically it is as if all the time and whatever I am doing, be it reading, working, planning action or just looking around, a continuous stream of language is welling up inside me and flowing out through me and on to the world, so that the world is heavily plastered over with words. That is how the world becomes intelligible to us. Look at anything around you, and just watch the words falling on it like snowflakes. As the language flows through us, I said, we seek to put a little personal spin on it, so as to reshape the world a little and make it express the meanings and values we'd like to see in it. However, the vocabulary and the valuations that I receive don't come to me from nowhere. The vocabulary we've got, and with which we find the world seemingly-spontaneously getting clothed, is the accumulated result of the interpretations and evaluations of hundreds of generations of our predecessors. They in all their time thought they were doing their bit to change the world for the better. We inherit the outcome of all their linguistic usages. We stand in a tradition, and the price we must pay for our ability to bend it a little is that our own interpretations and evaluations will themselves one day give rise to dissatisfaction, and get bent in their turn. So there is no single great overall project of world-redemption.

However, we are not altogether directionless. The most powerful redescribers and revaluers of the world, the great artists, do get remembered and do retain, it seems almost indefinitely, their power to refresh our feelings and our senses, and so to enhance life. Secondly, there is a standing ethical criterion that calls upon us to create and democratize value. For if our life has no outside, the values of life are intrinsic. That is, life's not for the sake of anything else, so we must love it for its own sake. And the best way to enhance the value of life for everyone is so to bend the language as to give as many things and people and aspects of our life as is coherently possible a better name. Much ethical activity in the modern period accordingly takes the form of a battle to upgrade some class of people or feature of our environment which has hitherto been unnecessarily low-rated. Hence campaigns and pressure-groups. And, I am arguing, it is rational to attempt in this way to democratize value, spreading it around more extensively and so raising the overall value of life for everyone. Indeed a movement towards democratization is, as Hegel noticed, often found in the history of politics and in the history of religions.

We do then have at least minimal guidelines for our attempts to transform the world that we receive. But so complex, so ambiguous and so outsideless is the human scene that we would do well to give up any idea of making overall progress. For that we'd need an independent, unchanging yardstick; and there is nowhere for such a yardstick to come from. So we need to be a little ironical about our own action, as well as about our own knowledge. Our values, like our theories, must be open to revision. We must, says Kierkegaard somewhere, strive with all our might in the knowledge that all our striving is but a jest.

After the affirmation of the life and the life-world that are continually given to us, and the attempt to transform the world a little by upgrading something or other, comes the third element in a religious attitude to life, a continual self-giving and *surrender* of our own life into the ongoing life of the world. We are transient products of the whole who have emerged from it, can contribute something to it, and must in due course be merged back into it. All through our lives our expressive and communicative activity flows out of us and into the public domain, where it promptly ceases to be in any way under our control. All our words and deeds are like children that must grow up and leave us. Our whole life is a process of letting go, letting go, letting go. A dying life, religion calls this, and a hard thing it is to accept. Joyfully and without regret or hesitation to relinquish our grudges, achievements, anxieties, children, vanities, possessions, ambitions, and whatever else we may be required to give up; this is extraordinarily difficult. It is a kind of preparation for death. But religion says that the more fully we accept that we are just a transient product of the world and destined to be merged back into it, the more spiritually free and joyful we become. Religious teachings about salvation and eternal life all turn on this paradox. If you are afraid of death and seek to save yourself from the world and protect your own selfhood, then your life will be dominated by anxiety and fear. But if you are able continually to let your own expression flow out of you and away into the world, without regret or holding back, then you will be liberated. To lose your life in this way is to save it. Life pours itself out all the time; we should do the same. To live is to pour oneself out in expressive communication, that is, to die. So life and death are the two faces of one reality, eternal life, or love.

In an age which recognizes the secondariness of consciousness, we have suggested, it is appropriate that the transient bit of us that is conscious should take up a religious attitude towards the larger background of life-expressing-itself-as-language of which we and our world are products. The religious object may be called life, or may be symbolized as the God of language. The appropriate religious attitude weaves together strands of affirmation, transformation and surrender. Where these three strands are properly developed, balanced and conjoined, a certain blessedness and freedom is still possible, even to us, even to us.

We are, by historical standards at least, metaphysically agnostic. Still, we have offered in outline a naturalistic interpretation of what religion was in the past, and may become today: a spirituality of world-making, after nihilism.

V

LANGUAGE AND THE SELF

1. Thinking in words

What people grandly call discursive conceptual thought can (so we have been suggesting) be redescribed without loss as a movement of incompletely-executed sentences somewhere in our organism. Concepts are just words, and thought is an ordering of words into sentences. True, people produce sentences which seem to suggest that concepts are non-physical things like tiny spirit-diagrams, and that thinking is a grinding of spirit-machinery; but such talk is metaphorical. It remains language. It does not take us into an immaterial realm outside language. There is no such realm. How could there be? We cannot possibly say what sort of change the conversion of sentences into non-linguistic thoughts might be, and looking at the opposite process, we cannot say how we could ever tell whether certain sentences do or do not accurately embody the non-linguistic thoughts behind them. And indeed it is very noticeable that a number of markedly different metaphors are used to portray the relation of thought to language. Words represent, articulate, express and convey thoughts. The very diversity of these metaphors shows that we don't in fact have a clear extra-linguistic notion of an extra-linguistic mental realm. On the contrary, mind is a complex metaphorical construction, something produced within and by language. And thinking is therefore a *sotto voce* talking to oneself, a kind of inner soliloquy. We think fastest when we are thinking what to say next, just because thinking is, and is only, a taking-shape of sentences. And, I am suggesting, just as in these sentences of mine 'thought' and 'thinking' are just words that can only be explained in more words, so it is also in your head. There too you can find only words always leading on to more words. True, the words may seem to conjure up pictures, for example of an inner space; but the inner space is only a metaphor and therefore remains a function of the language that evokes it. The inner space cannot ever get to be more than a linguistic metaphor. It is only an as-if conjured up by the way the words move, and cannot get to be a real space surrounding the words and within which they move. We cannot step clear of language to picture inner space as a special kind of non-spatial space wherein real and non-metaphorical trains of thought clank to and fro. We do not have any non-metaphorical and extra-linguistic ways of representing the mind and what goes on within it. Between an incoming sentence and an outgoing one, what can we interpose? Only more sentences, about 'the mind' as a telephone-exchange or a computer. So 'the mind' is always a metaphor, an epiphenomenon of language.

Very well: but surely the sheer abundance in the language of these metaphors of the mental shows that we do at least entertain mental images? In which case thinking is not only a movement of language, but also involves inner pictures. Inner space, mental machinery, introspection, trains of thought, an inner world of the imagination – these phrases seem to generate pictures. As the sentences shunt in and out of our heads they certainly do seem to us to be projecting flickering mental pictures upon the dark walls of our minds. And don't we in any case need to postulate an interior stock of non-linguistic mental pictures in order to account for our own ability to recognize places and faces? I cannot describe my friend James sufficiently accurately in words, so my capacity to recognize him instantly cannot be stored in the form of a verbal description. It must surely take the form of a mental picture.

Unfortunately, the notion of a picture library in my head through which I search, looking for a mugshot to match the person who has just come in, is once again yet another linguistic metaphor. We have recognitional capacities indeed, but whether they are portrayed as being filing systems, data banks, picture libraries or whatever is just a matter of fashions in words. All that is given is a behavioural capacity: when James comes in I am able to say 'James!' Asked to explain this feat, I cannot do more than call up the currently-popular metaphor. I never actually get to make a direct comparison between two pictures, the one of James presenting himself in person, and the other from my mental file. Mental pictures are metaphors. They are not real pictures. They are not things *seen*, at all.

So I do not need to qualify the initial thesis very much. It was that all discursive conceptual thought is transacted in language and depends upon it. We add that there are various special artificial languages in which people can think, such as the languages of mathematics and music. I do not deny that people such as painters, sculptors, mechanical engineers and film directors have, as it were, special skills of entertaining and manipulating shapes, colours and sequences. And we have also certain recognitional skills. But I still wish to say that all these skills are also language-dependent. Language provides the material basis for our capacity consciously to seem-to-entertain images, to manipulate them, to order them in sequence, and to use them to make symbolic statements. Mental images or pictures are not real images or pictures, and nobody will ever produce one. They are language-evoked metaphors and no more. The vocabulary in which we speak of mental phenomena is so vivid that it seems to be describing a reveal inner space, but it is merely evoking such a space by metaphor. Furthermore, humour, word-play and creativity real to us that our unconscious thinking is just as completely transacted in language as is our conscious thought. So 'the mind' is a way of symbolizing our participation in language, and the inner mental space of subjectivity is just the roominess of language itself. Language makes you feel you have an inside, of course. But that 'inside' is only a metaphor, a creation of language. So our subjective consciousness is a product of language or culture.

So much for the thesis. Here are eight supporting arguments.

First, there are many indications that thought is an internalization of speech. For it seems manifestly the case that mental arithmetic is a secondary internalization of a skill that was first acquired outwardly with pencil and paper, that reading silently to oneself is a secondary refinement of the skill of reading aloud that we were taught, and that silent prayer is an internalization of praying aloud. In all these cases and in others like them too, we first had to learn to perform visibly and audibly, and then we learnt the knack of inhibiting and privatizing our performance so that it seemed to us to be taking place in an inner theatre of subjective consciousness. All of which suggests that thinking generally is a silent soliloquy, suppressed speech. Conversely, thinking 'out loud' again is just talking.

Secondly, although a tradition thousands of years old makes people want to picture thinking as an immaterial activity that goes on outside language, we are in fact quite unable to represent thinking as being anything else but a movement of language. If I say, 'A penny for your thoughts!', I am asking for some sentences. Similarly, we cannot represent a concept as being anything but just a word, the form of consecutive thought as being anything but syntax, or the difference between two thoughts in any terms but those of language. So what, *other* than a movement of language, can anyone suppose that thought might consist in? There is no other stuff for thought to be made of.

The third argument is that our being of like mind and able to communicate successfully with each other is better understood if we put the common language first and treat individual subjectivities as so many privatizations of it than if we begin within one subjectivity, such as my own, and then try to get across to others. Certainly, a long tradition in philosophy thought it possible as-it-were to bracket off the question of language, and to begin within one's own subjectivity. Starting within the sphere of my private experience, I was supposed to be able to work my way out into the public world, to identify other centres of subjective experience and to establish communication with them. But even supposing I manage to do all this successfully, there remains a haunting doubt. How can I be sure that the thoughts and feelings that I encoded into the language I have just transmitted are being faithfully reproduced in the other thoughts and feelings into which the receiver at the far end decodes my sentences? Is there not always a possibility of systematic misunderstanding? And this uneasy suspicion has arisen, I am suggesting, because we started in the wrong place. Our being of like mind and able to communicate successfully with each other is something so vital to our survival that Nature has taken no chances with it. The public domain comes first. You and I are both native speakers of the same language. You are one local privatization of it, and I am another. One and the same language that pervades our entire social world runs through your head and runs also through mine. Our likemindedness and capacity for mutual understanding are therefore secured by the public character of linguistic meaning.

Fourthly, it has come to be recognized in modern times that every human being is culturally programmed. Nobody's mind is ever a blank slate. We are always within a particular complex construction of the world, valuation of life and (as Rorty calls it) 'final vocabulary'.[1] But how is this cultural programming, which gives us our cultural identity, imposed upon us? Because everyone is and has to be a member of a language-group, because a person's own identity is bound up with her mother-tongue, because culture is undeniably intimately linked to language, because language is never a neutral communication-medium but is always very highly ideologically-loaded, and because we learn language in idioms, in language-games and cultural practices, for all these reasons we can treat language and culture as coextensive and effectively coinciding. A living language is always cultural, in that it is freighted with a set of local valuations and practices. Learning the language, we learn the local customs and assumptions. So the programming within which our identity is constituted is in effect our linguistic programming, our induction into the network of human communication.

Fifthly, Freud found that sometimes a person hysterically mute in her or his own language is nevertheless able to function in a foreign language. This observation has since developed into the occasional use of foreign languages as therapeutic tools. Clinical experience indicates that the mother-tongue is especially emotionally-fraught. We are cooler when we switch to French or German. But this demonstrates that we do not think and feel in extra-linguistic signified thoughts or feelings. On the contrary, our feelings and thoughts are tied to the verbal signifiers of a particular vocabulary. All our deepest and most intense associations and feelings are tied expressly to *Mutter* and not to *Mother* (or whatever the case may be). Thought is, then, 'semiotic materialist'. Like jokes, puns and crossword puzzle clues, it turns on the material characteristics of words. When we say that the personality is constituted within language, we mean that a human personality is a particular manner in which a whole lot of material linguistic signifiers move in relation to each other.

My sixth argument for the entirely-linguistic character of thought is that the *perpetuum mobile* or endlessly-running character of thought is best understood as produced by, and as consisting in, the endlessness of language and interpretation. In thought, one thing leads to another and so on forever, just as it does in the dictionary and in the literature of any topic. Every word gets its meaning from the way it moves relative to other words. Every meaning is a difference. So every word leads me on to more words. And that is what thought is: endless digression and excursus.

Which leads me to my seventh argument. In spite of what Descartes and so many other philosophers have suggested, our thinking is only very partially under our control. Introspectively, as we lie in bed relaxed, thought is an endless scurrying-about of rather fragmentary and ill-lit sentences, only a very few of which we can follow through. That is the language dynamo, to which we referred earlier. It is libidinally-driven and automobile. I do not *compose* these sentences; I feel them running around over a surface. Thought is a remembering, a rehearsing, a simulation, an entertaining, a play and a letting-rip of language.

Out of this prodigious wealth, we select; who knows how?

But my eighth and last argument for the identification of thought with a motion of material signifiers is that by 'a clear thinker' we just mean, and can only mean, someone who is able to produce a string of clear and well-formed sentences that are to the point.

If these arguments are sound, then the whole of our life is lived inside the flux of language and history. Language comes first. It is written into the unconscious in a way of which Jacques Lacan was the first to make us fully aware. English Darwinians, at least when they read Freud, are inclined to read him as suggesting that the Unconscious is a cauldron of seething, inordinate biological drives, complicated no doubt by traumas, repressions, memories and propensities to symbolize in this way or that, but nonetheless basically biological, pre-cultural and extra-linguistic. But Lacan helps us to see how completely we are constituted within language and culture by demonstrating that the Unconscious is already through-and-through linguistic, and that Freud himself needs to be read as showing this. All the material presented to Freud was linguistic – reports of dreams, the results of association tests, symbolic actions, jokes and so forth – and his method of working was always more like literary criticism than natural science. Nobody has as yet quite done for Jung what Lacan did for Freud, but the message must clearly be the same. We are constituted within culture and language – and not merely at the conscious level, either. Our deep biological constitution has always been so imbued by language that the feelings we have and the way they come into expression, as well as all our perceptual and cognitive capacities, are all formed by cultural signs. So we are made of words all the way down.

Why did people ever think otherwise? It seems that much of philosophy up to Kant took a supernaturalist view of the mind, reason, concepts, truth, meaning and 'pure thought'. All these things could somehow exist outside language, and did so. Thomas Aquinas never asks in precisely what language the angels communicate with each other. They spoke to Dante in Italian. Did Dante really suppose that one could hear Italian spoken in Heaven? The question of language in the hereafter does not seem even to

have been asked before Swedenborg, who answers as might be
expected of an eighteenth-century writer, that there is

> . . . a universal language proper to all angels and spirits, which
> has nothing in common with any language spoken in the world.
> Every man, after death, uses this language, for it is implanted in
> everyone from creation; and therefore throughout the whole
> spiritual world all can understand one another. I have frequently
> heard this language and, having compared it with languages
> in the world, have found that . . . it differs from them in this
> fundamental respect, that every letter of every word has a
> particular meaning. That is why God is called the Alpha and the
> Omega . . .[2]

As compared with the 'positive' or locally-evolved languages of
earth, Swedenborg is saying, the absolute language is universal,
unchanging and innate, like 'natural religion' or 'the natural moral
law'. He also explains in detail that both in its written and in its
spoken forms it has a qualitatively-greater expressive power than
any earthly language has. There is more meaning in the letters and
more love in the tone. So at least Swedenborg assures us, and we
should certainly not smile at him. Despite his spectacular eccentri-
cities he belongs to the Enlightenment and has asked a perfectly
sensible question. If Heaven is a society, it must have a language.
Which – and how do we get to learn it? The questions multiply.
A society must communicate, communication requires language,
and language seems to presuppose bodies to vibrate, a fluid
medium to carry soundwaves, and a hard surface to bear graphic
signs. So what kind of language can discarnate spirits be supposed
to use?

At least in the tradition based on Greek philosophy, the presumption seems to have been that God, the angels, and disem-
bodied human souls think non-linguistically and communicate
telepathically. The pre-philosophical view had been that God just
spoke Hebrew, or Arabic, or whatever else was thought to be the
language in which he had from all eternity composed the scriptures. Everyone in heaven would presumably therefore need to

speak the language God spoke. Philosophy finds this view too mythological, and postulates 'thought' as a universal spiritual language. This very advantageously distances God and philosophy from the contingency and the limitations of the material linguistic signifier and local cultures. It makes possible the impressive show of generality and authority that is still so conspicuous even in Kant's writing, where it is as if the philosopher's writing is not mere writing but Thought, the language of Heaven, pure and universal.

Two centuries later, though, we have become aware of how odd the older kind of realistic dogmatic theology and philosophy was. It was founded on a systematic exclusion of language and culture from direct attention. By special literary devices it created an appearance of transcending the literary; it was a local feigning of universal truth. The most important of these literary devices was the elaboration of a mentalistic vocabulary which evoked the notion of pure thought. Thought was made to seem like a universal spiritual-language-of-the-mind, underlying the various phonic-and-graphic, culturally-evolved languages of human beings, and even shared with the spirit-world. I was made in the image of God, so I could think God's thoughts after him. The self and God transcended human language *together*. Just as human thought was supposed to transcend the language in which it was conducted, so God was supposed to transcend the analogies and metaphors of religious language. The material linguistic utterance was therefore paralleled by a higher-level spiritual communication between God and the mind. Really proficient souls were able, for example in wordless contemplative prayer, to drop human language. When I engaged in sustained non-linguistic thought I was like an angel, using God's own language. So the true universal language of which Swedenborg speaks, the language 'proper to all angels and spirits' which we will all speak after we are dead, was the language of pure thought itself. For, I am suggesting, our human languages have built into them, and keep conjuring up, the suggestion that pure discursive thought is not conducted in our everyday human language. It must employ a universal spiritual language of Reason-itself, the language of God and the heavenly world. Such was the implicit belief, for centuries, of Western thinkers.

Conversely, however, if we have succeeded in showing that all our human 'thinking' is a movement of words and sentences in our ordinary human language,[3] then the corollaries and consequences are very considerable indeed.

2. Impure thought

The realization that we are constituted as subjects entirely within a local human language, and therefore also within culture and within history, is a great event. It brings to an end a supernaturalist view of ourselves which we had clung to tenaciously for as long as we possibly could.

For example, the best nineteenth-century phrenological busts were made by L. N. Fowler. The way they show the various mental faculties distributed over the cranium gives a vivid insight into the values of the period. We are not at all surprised to find that the dead-centre summit of the cranial dome, the very crown of the head, is marked 'Worship'. Immediately before it are Benevolence and Spirituality, and just behind it are Hope, Conscientiousness and Firmness. These are what the age called 'Man's moral and religious capacities', and Fowler makes them literally the highest functions of the brain. Even Charles Darwin's closest friends and allies balked at the suggestion that such lofty spiritual faculties might have a merely this-worldly origin. What of the capacity for speech? It is situated at the front of the head, indeed, but at the very lowest level. It is even below the sense of sight, for 'Language' and 'Verbal expression' are printed on the lower eyelid. The only other mental faculties equally low-rated are the desire for food and drink, printed around the earlobe, and 'Love of sex', inscribed at the cloaca of the skull, the point where the spinal column enters it.

The suggestion here that where matters of sex are concerned people are not quite in their right minds is no doubt understandable, but it is perplexing and instructive to find language being rated equally low. We are intended to gather than the great bulk of our mental activity transcends language. Thought is spiritual. It is regulated by culture-transcending and timeless standards.

The traditional realism of Western culture required us to believe that the moral, religious and intellectual standards we live by transcend history, transcend culture and transcend every natural human language. To recognize these standards and to be guided by them, therefore, the human mind had to be mostly outside language. On Fowler's phrenological bust you are immersed in the relativities of language and culture and history only up to the level of your eyes. Above that level you are an angel. That noble forehead and crowned dome of yours sticks out of both nature and culture. It inhabits a noumenal world of timeless verities, at which you gaze with your 'mind's eye'.

All this calls for some explanation, because in the Bible – or at least, in the Hebrew Bible and in the stories about Jesus in the Synoptic Gospels – it seems to be readily accepted that what people call thought is just language moving in the heart. Men reason within their hearts, and say within themselves.[4] God's spirit speaks within our hearts, and God writes in the heart. But in the philosophical tradition which stems from Greece there has been all the way through – and most especially in the early modern period, from Descartes to Kant – an unacknowledged but systematic repression of the thought that thought is just a movement of language. The extent to which great thinkers composed in language texts which refuse to advert to the question of language is extraordinary. Why?

The case of Descartes is relatively clear. He was concerned to find a rationale for the new mathematical physics. The mind that constructed a representation of the world as being rigorously mechanistic had to distance itself from the machine it described. The mind had to be like a spirit, a disengaged observer. It gazed upon the world in a contemplative manner, and as if from outside. Its representation of the material world in knowledge was constructed *in a medium that was different in kind*. The mind–matter gap was as big as the God-world gap. Descartes could not accept the pragmatist view that human knowledge is also part of nature, being always bound up with human interests and purposes and with social interactions and practical activities, because that would immediately raise the question of how in a deterministic universe freedom of thought and action are possible. So in his *Meditations* he pictures the thinker as being like a solitary angel who views the world from outside, constructing objective knowledge of himself, God and the world in pure thought. But Descartes can only do this by writing in such a way as systematically to conceal from himself and from us the question of writing. As we follow his doubts through to the 'I exist' it must not occur to us that he is using language and that language is always already material and social, or the illusion would be punctured.[5]

In Descartes' case, then, the belief that thoughts are spiritual goings-on in our minds that are in principle prior to and independent of the materiality of language was needed in order to defend the possibility of objective man-made scientific knowledge of a mechanistic universe. Even to this day, most scientists remain scientific realists who believe in the traditional supernaturalism of thought. They have to keep up this implausible view in order to sustain the claim that Nature and the scientific knowledge of Nature can together be prior to and so can escape the relativities of language and history and culture. Science privileges itself, trying to establish its own autonomy. Scientists maintain the Cartesian supernaturalism of thought in order to maintain a supernaturalism of scientific knowledge. The outstanding case is that of the various cognitive and psychological sciences. These people do not want 'the mind' to be de-centred and to disappear into the play of language and the relativities of cultural and historical difference and change. It is a professional necessity that they should have a subject matter to study and that it should stay in place. But neither can they permit 'the mind' to become just a deterministic machine, just a collection of material processes, or they would lose their own *locus standi* for constructing and evaluating their theories about it. Professionally, they need there to be such a thing as the mind. It must stay in place, *and* it must be possible for it to construct properly scientific theories about itself that it can test and evaluate freely. The mind thus has to be both 'natural' and 'free', both a sort of machine and a sort of Cartesian spirit. These conflicting metaphysical pre-conditions for the existence of such a subject as Cognitive Science determine the type of language that must be used in it. Psychologists have to believe in subjective experience, mental imagery and mental processes. They have to believe that there is an extra-linguistic realm of inner mental 'machinery' that is both material enough for it to be appropriate to set out to frame testable scientific hypotheses about it, and yet at the same time 'free', Cartesian and spiritual enough for it to be able to test and evaluate these physicalizing theories *about itself*!

If it is difficult to see how all this can be true at once, it is even more difficult for science to accept that it is itself a cultural construction. When science accepts that it is always done within language and always presupposes language, then it is decentred. It loses its innocence. There ceases to be any pure access to pure Nature, independent of culture. Thought, sense-experience and theorizing cease to be pure. *Truth* ceases to be pure. This is not easy to accept. Scientists may perhaps be able to admit it in relation to the science of the past. A large literature has demonstrated that, for example, nineteenth-century medical men, in their pronouncements about such vital topics as Woman, insanity, adolescence, childbirth and so forth, were enforcing purely local cultural values. They thought that what they were saying was 'scientific', in the sense of being naturally and extra-culturally True, but in retrospect it is clear that they were acting as cultural policemen. Nobody considering the evidence could today deny that much or most of nineteenth-century medicine has thus been decentred, in the sense that it has been shown that it was something rather different from what it thought it was. But *today's* life sciences and human sciences do not find it easy to accept that in all probability their own pretensions will one day be similarly decentred by a retrospective gaze.

3. The Last Judgement

Many religions teach both that God has ordained and still upholds the entire set-up under which we live, and that he will nevertheless shortly come to deliver a devastating judgment upon it and terminate it forever. This is a strange doctrine. Why should an omniscient God need to carry out a minute and comprehensive audit of states of affairs that are by definition wide open to his gaze already, and how do we know in advance that his verdict, upon an order of things that he personally established and still appears to condone, is so sure to be hostile? Yet from another angle all is not quite so paradoxical as it may at first seem, for the one best qualified to judge the world is surely the one who created it in the first place and who must therefore know where all the hiding-places are. Besides, it is somehow inevitable that the object of our deepest apprehensions must coincide with the object of our most fervent appeals for help. Religious language shows it. In a whole series of exclamations and expletives the word *God* is used to link together widely disparate emotional responses to life: *Thank God!, O God!, God damn it!, My God!, God help us!, Good God!* To call such phrases mere swearwords is too shallow. They are serious religious exclamations, through which our feelings about life can be expressed forcibly and made cosmic. A number of other terms – *It* or *Things* or, indeed, *Life* itself – are also used in the standard idioms that express how we feel about the way of things and how it is treating us, but *God* is the most potent. It draws out, focusses and unifies our feelings more powerfully than other words can do.

In this way then the word 'God' becomes the central symbol of religion. 'God' is just an outburst, an expression of our highest hopes, our worst terrors, our most universal values. God is the religious concern and the expressed religious response to life. That being so, the ancient doctrine that God is both the Creator of the current set-up and its Judge may be seen as symbolizing an inevitable and permanent duality or ambiguity in the religious response to life. We say a wholehearted Yes to the existing order of things, even while at the very same time we are also attempting to re-negotiate it or to transform it. We bless *and* we curse. We are both satisfied and dissatisfied, both world-affirming and world-denying, both 'conservative' and 'radical', both attached and detached, both aesthetes who are content to accept things as they are and moralists who want things to be different.

Talk of God as Creator and Judge functions, therefore, to evoke a spiritual stance or attitude to life which we should maintain all the time. This stance is at once affirmative all the way through and critical all the way through. The Creation-theme calls for a permanent policy of world-acceptance, while simultaneously the Judgment-theme calls for a permanent policy of comprehensive world-criticism. We acknowledge that our world is ours. We made it. We ourselves built up the language and the culture by which we are programmed. God – the life-giving, outpouring and world-making power of language – is continuously creating our world through us. Our programming, that is, our language, our action and our habits of perception are all the time construct-ing our world. It all flows out of us, and yet even as we acknow-ledge all this and say 'Yes' to it, we also feel dissatisfied with the world that we have made and are still making, and we seek to change it.

In our culture the criticism of knowledge and of social institu-tions is by now well-established. As we grasp the extent to which through our language, our theory and our action we are all the time constructing our world, we begin to see the need for world-criticism. The old religious ideas of divine Creation and Judgment were forerunners of the more recent insights.

If along these lines we demythologize the old idea of a Last Judgment, we have a possible starting-point for a philosophy of post-historical existence, something that is at present urgently needed. After so many centuries we Westerners find it very hard to do without a narrative meaning of life. We need to feel we are part of a story – and preferably a *long* story. The typically post-modern compression of everything into the elusive, deferred, non-present present moment is very disorienting to us. But, I shall argue, religion too knows about that compression, and has its own version of it.

The doctrine of a catastrophic 'Day of the Lord' is of uncertain origin, but appears to go back at least to the Israelite prophets of the eighth century BCE.[7] It developed into all the immensely-influential eschatological doctrines, found in ancient Iranian religion[8] as well as among Jews, Christians, Muslims and others, which have portrayed world history as moving step by step towards a future consummation. Such doctrines have taken many different forms. Originally the main emphasis was upon God's over-riding control of all historical events, his covenant, his warnings, his threats and his promises, his eternal will and his predestinating decree. But out of the great theological systems there developed also many secular versions of the doctrine. They pictured humanity as being progressively liberated by the growth of knowledge, by necessary political and social developments, by the increasing power of technology and so on. They were, in short, secular myths of redemption. They taught much of the human race to believe that something or other says that the future must be better than the past, and so have been used to inspire and legitimate democratic politics, scientific research, social reform, industrial development, economic growth and much else besides. In one way and another the secular myths of redemption have encouraged people to believe that world-history-as-a-whole is like a very large but tightly constructed narrative, in which all events have been designed by the author to make some contribution towards the resolution of the whole plot. To believe that my life has a meaning was to believe that my doings are scripted, essential parts of a vast ongoing narrative with a preordained happy ending. God is working his purpose out, and history is getting somewhere. It will end with a bang. The moral accounts will be audited, the books will be balanced, and people will get their deserts.

It is often said that the belief in progress got killed off by the horrors of the two World Wars, or by the discovery of environmental limits to growth. That is, twentieth-century bad news was so extra bad that it falsified the over-optimistic beliefs of earlier and more innocent ages. But this cannot be right. There have always been horrors, and the idea of limits to growth is certainly not new. No, the really decisive new cultural fact of the modern period has been the crucial and irreversible realization, first that myth is myth, and secondly, that the myths of the Enlightenment were also myths. That is, all our stories about progress, about liberation, about redemption are cultural products. We made them. They are not part of the eternal order of things, because there *is* no eternal order of things. And when did we come to see this? Roughly speaking, although the Enlightenment believed itself to be demythologized, in fact it merely replaced old religious myths with new and very similar secular myths about Reason, Truth, Progress, Enlightenment and so forth. But during the late nineteenth century there began to take place the event that really mattered, the Second Demythologizing, as it came to be realized that all the beliefs of the Enlightenment had been mythical too.

The second demythologizing is a fatality, traumatic, unstoppable and inexcusable. It is a turning-point. When it has occurred, Karl Marx looks much the same as St Augustine. Frankly, there's little to choose between them. Compared with where we now are, Marx is mediaeval. He is a realist, in the sense that he believes that there is a nature of things. In particular, there is a nature of history, for Marx thinks we are all acting roles in a drama already scripted for us by the laws of historical development. He thinks he is telling us how it is, but for us there *is* no how it is, and Marx is only recommending certain myths, interpretations, policies and readings of his own. That means that if we are still Marxists, we can be only ironical, non-realistic Marxists. Dogmatic Marxist faith is no longer an option, because dogmatism requires a kind of projection of cultural conceptions out into objectivity, and we can no longer make ourselves unaware that we are doing that.

Now the end of dogmatism or realism is also the end of history, insofar as for many centuries 'history' has meant the belief in something out there which generates a story and works to ensure that the future marks an advance upon the past. If there is nothing out there to make the future better than the past, and not even anything there by reference to which we will be able to tell whether the future is any better or worse than the past, then our historical strivings and sufferings seem to lose their justification and their aim. It seems that we no longer have any measure of where things are or should be going, nor of whether we are getting there.

Is this a major event? In some countries, every Tom, Dick and Harriet will assure you that of course they are not so naive as to believe in progress. If they are right, the end of belief in an object-ive Arrow pointing forwards, onwards and upwards is a minor matter. But they are *not* right. Western economies still depend upon people's belief that this year's products are or should be an advance upon last year's. That is to say, we buy the new products because we have been persuaded that they are more subtly tailored to meet our needs and gratify our desires than last year's products were. Similarly, liberal democracy depends upon the voters' belief that their elected representatives can deliver something identifiable as social progress. Science and technology get funded and are pursued on the basis of the belief that in proportion to the money and effort invested science will progressively approximate towards objective knowledge of the way the world really is. It is thought that this knowledge once gained will be highly beneficial to us, because pure objective knowledge, rationally applied in maximally-efficient technologies, really will make human life maximally blessed and happy. When all this is spelled out, it is indeed clear to us that we no longer believe in 'the perfectibility of man', as it was called. It has become difficult to see how the increase of scientific knowledge and technical skill can of them-selves create Heaven on earth, and it has become difficult politically to see beyond liberal democracy and a perpetual struggle to al-leviate people's sufferings and arbitrate their conflicts. Nothing necessitates the withering away of the state and the arrival of a fully-achieved communist society. To that extent, it is obvious that we no longer believe in progress.

Yet we clearly haven't yet been able to come to terms with our own loss of faith. Why else are we still buying new products, believing politicians and funding research? As a society, we are not yet quite ready for post-historical existence. In post-history we are going to have to pursue science, social reform and product-change autonomously and just for art's sake, without believing that things are getting any better overall. We are going to need a politics of stability, a cyclical environmental politics, that is not morally indolent. And it seems that we are not prepared intellectually or morally for aimlessness, life without an Arrow pointing onwards and upwards. Individuals, no doubt, can do it. A keen potter for example may live without thought for the morrow, absorbed in an eternal present. She can keep on striving and innovating, and does not need to believe that she is getting anywhere. But it is not yet clear how a whole science-based industrial economy is going to learn to live like that.

That is why I am suggesting that a non-narrative but still religious attitude to life, which somehow manages to fuse together world-acceptance and restless world-criticism, is highly relevant to the times. In religion the challenge is – and I have been arguing that it can be met – to give up thinking in terms of a creation-event in the past, a God up there guiding things, and a future End of history, and instead accept the compression of everything into the moment. The feasts are spread out over the liturgical year, but if they are questioned, believers will acknowledge that of course Christ is born all the time, dies and is risen every day. It's all true all the time. Breaking it up and spreading it out is done merely for didactic reasons. And the same is true of theology generally.

Merleau-Ponty and a string of other Continental philosophers have said that a philosophical ideology does not exist for its own sake, but for the sake of the stream of life-experience from which it was abstracted and into which it must return.[9] Similarly, theology too is for the sake of life. We tend to project out a narrative framework: a Creation in the past, standards out there, a drama of salvation, a God above and a Goal of history in the future. But actually all this material exists only for the sake of the stream of present lived experience and action. The imposing scheme of doctrine was developed only to shape and to guide the stream of life.[10] The dogmas of Creation and Judgment seem at first sight to be very grand and cosmic. But, I have argued, they can easily be given an attitudinal interpretation. They do not have to be narrative or objective. To believe in the doctrine of Creation is in a certain way to say 'Yes' to life and to accept life as a gift. To believe in a Last Judgment is to think critically (*crisis* = judgment): to live as one under judgment in a world that is under judgment, to live an examined, accountable, responsible sort of a life. And I am saying of these grand cosmic themes of Creation and Judgment not only that they are patient of an attitudinal and regulative interpretation as life-guiding pictures, but also that that is all that they can possibly mean anyway, because it is blindingly obvious that nothing exists but the here and now, and that all faiths, philosophies and ideologies are in the end just traffic-management proposals dreamt up by way of ordering and shaping the stream of life in the here and now. So why are we so alarmed by the recent collapse of the great stories? Why do so many, even of the best of us, feel that life is worthless and empty unless we can really believe that we are playing a part in a Grand Narrative?

4. *Life stories*

Now she has Alzheimer's. I recall her as she was, doting on her children, smiling just a little mischievously as she watched her husband holding forth, presiding in her own domain. But now she, *she* has Alzheimer's, and I feel a certain frigid distaste for the whole subject of life's casual brutality. What is there to be said about something so utterly irremediable? Better, surely, to imitate the matter-of-fact fatalism of the Homeric heroes, as so many ordinary, courageous people do. After the first blow we stagger, shake ourselves, and go on. After the second we fall, and take a while to get to our feet again. After the third, we drop and remain still. That's how it all ends, as everyone knows. Complaint is superfluous. Now let's talk about the good times.

There is a view held by certain extreme elitists of the Right, that the manifest and familiar truth about human life cannot be endured by the vast majority of human beings.[11] In a sense people can hardly be unaware that our little Earth is surrounded by billions of light years of death in all directions and that the Universe at large is totally indifferent to values and consciousness. One day, the last human being will perish and universal night will descend. The facts about old age, mortality, transience and the Void are non-narrative, natural and certain. But only a tiny minority of philosophers and artists are able to look straight at these facts, deriving from them in the one case a certain detached and calm intellectual pleasure, and in the other a stimulus to creativity. The rest of humanity will never be able to bear the truth. They have to be surrounded by protective narratives and rituals in order to survive and be made sober enough to be governable.

From this point of view, religion is the social institution that makes all other social institutions possible. Religion gives the people a narrative meaning for their lives. Its great myths of divine creation, divine providence, sin and redemption assuage people's primal terror in the face of the Void, calm their desires, discipline them, and make them industrious and manageable. Religion is a political necessity. Indeed, it alone can make most human animals something like rational. And because, furthermore, philosophers also need the stable social conditions that religion alone can create, the wise will always support it in their exoteric teaching. Privately, the philosophers hold very different views and find their own ways of communicating with each other. But they must not make the mistake of supposing that general enlightenment is either possible or desirable. The philosophers have always been enlightened; the masses must never become so.

The great error of modern society has been the attempt, since the French Revolution, to democratize enlightenment. Through the criticism of religion, the diffusion of scientific naturalism and the demystification of the social order and the moral order, modern intellectuals have tried to teach the people truths which in the past philosophers wisely kept to themselves. The result has been intellectual and moral chaos, with widespread *anomie* and social unrest. The people's desires run out of control. They start expecting too much. In weak countries there are regular coups: in strong countries the state's administrative control of life has to be expanded enormously in order to make up for the weakening of the old religious sanctions.

To restore stability we probably need the sort of educational reforms that the Right was attempting to introduce during the 1980s. We don't want the diffusion through the population of critical and speculative thinking. We want a culture based on an alliance between technology and neo-conservative religion. There will always be a tiny elite of philosophers, who may have some links with the highest-ranking technocrats. But they and their views will not be known to the public. So far as the general public is concerned, the culture will consist of technology plus fundamentalism, together with plenty of innocuous entertainment.

Technology, fundamentalism, entertainment; and philosophy permanently invisible. That, perhaps, is what's coming. In some places it seems to have arrived already, and from the point of view I am describing it is the optimal solution. Philosophers should support it.

Everything here depends upon a clear distinction between two levels of teaching and two sorts of truth. The esoteric teaching conveys a truth which is primary, natural, certain, non-narrative, and unbearable except by the philosophers, who love it. The exoteric or public doctrine is secondary, narrative, illusory and politically necessary for the people.

The esoteric or secret doctrine is a body of truths conveyed in the writings of such as Hume, Schopenhauer, Darwin, Nietzsche, Russell and Sartre, but about which they were rather more explicit than they should have been. We are talking here about a very odd reverse-Gnosticism. What is being charitably veiled from the masses is not a secret body of hard-to-discover Good News, but a body of blindingly-obvious Bad News about their own true condition. It is the philosophical elite who are able to live out in the open air and face the daylight, whereas it is the people who must live indoors and look at pictures. They have to have the painted curtain of narrative truth hung before their eyes: they cannot live without it.

Much could be said about this body of political doctrine. One may point out, for example, that the sharp distinction between esoteric truth for a tiny elite and exoteric truth for the people cannot be upheld. At a certain level all the people know and have always known the Bad News. Of course they do; how could they not? Religion itself requires us to pass through an encounter with the Bad News, in the Bible for example in the books of *Job*, *Ecclesiastes* and *St Mark*, and in the liturgical year on Good Friday and at funeral services. Furthermore, although the esoteric doctrine, the Bad News, professes to be non-narrative it naively provides the philosophers with a highly flattering story about themselves, by telling them that they are superlatively courageous and strong-minded people who can gaze tranquilly at truths that would destroy lesser mortals. This is laughably unjust to the courage and endurance of millions of ordinary people – and it shows that the thought of oneself as a person able to transcend the comforts of myth is itself a most gratifying myth.

But this brings us to the key issue. The Philosophical Right claim that myth, language and narrative do not go all the way down. There is a primary body of natural, certain truth about the human condition, and it is non-narrative. Because it is there, it makes narrative knowledge relatively illusory in comparison with it. The old Greek maxim is still in place: *Muthos* for the people, *Logos* for the philosophers. But the Greek doctrine has been moved on a stage. The new higher truth is the fearful secret that there is no secret, the grim truth that there is no Higher Truth and our life is (as the people would put it) 'utterly meaningless'. This truth must be kept from the people. They must go on believing their stories about a Higher Truth that has been vouchsafed to them.

Now as you may guess I am not blaming these doctrines of the old Philosophical hard Right for being excessively sceptical. On the contrary, they are not nearly sceptical enough. Not only are they self-serving and naively conceited, but also there is something badly wrong with the idea that there is an objective, certain, natural and non-narrative truth of things out there, which the wise contemplate.

What's wrong with this doctrine is that it once again invokes the old claim that thought can go beyond language. For the production of language is a bodily action, which always evokes, forms and expresses the body's emotional drives. The making of sentences is a passionate, exhausting business. The sentence is a vehicle whose range of possible forms has been prescribed by society, and which can therefore function as a channel for the discharge of a measure of body-energy as socially-intelligible action. Sentences express our feelings, aspirations, desires, wishes in significant forms. The subject-verb-object structure of the sentence is already a simple narrative. We are narrative animals. Narrative implies a certain expenditure of body-energy along a culturally-provided pathway, its 'meaning', so that every human expression and action can take on story-like significance.

An excellent example of the intimate parallelism between language and action is the radio commentary, for example on a football match. Or you can try providing a continuous running commentary upon your own actions as you perform them. You will soon find how easily and neatly human physical actions drop into sentence-shapes. During sex experienced lovers use language to trigger orgasm, a clear and simple case of the way words have the power to draw the body's drives forth into expression.

The way sentences are action-shaped and actions are sentence-shaped is well captured in Shakespeare's 'Suit the action to the word, the word to the action'.[12] It is also very prominent in scriptural religion, especially in the idea of living by the Book, turning written sentences directly into a way of life. Theology constantly strives to make as intimate as possible the relationship between words and deeds, faith and works, doctrine and life, the lips and the heart, the inward and the outward. In its slightly oblique way theology is saying that a human being is a very special sort of acculturated animal that lives by pouring out its feelings coded as meanings, and finding expression in sentence-actions. That's what we are; that's how we tick.

It follows that the traditional Philosophical life was illusory. Capital-P Philosophy claimed to practise a passion-less and objective contemplation of 'natural' or cosmic meanings and truths that are somehow out there and accessible quite apart from our language and our passions. But there is no such thing as this sexless languageless monstrosity, 'pure thought', and if there were such a thing it would certainly not be any concern of us human beings, who function only by pouring out our passions through those socially-conventionalized channels we call words.

If we reject the old belief in something called 'the mind' or 'thought', what are we rejecting, and how can we even formulate our rejection without falling into the very ways of 'thinking' that we repudiate? We will have to say that thoughts in minds were myths that arose because metaphors were taken too seriously, or were too crudely handled. Our mentalistic vocabulary is perfectly usable. I will even concede that it does a good job. But, historically, it is demonstrably only a lot of metaphors of metaphors. The thinking classes reified it by way of fictioning their own superiority to the common people. The home country of the intellectuals is a higher world, the world of thought, to which they are expert guides. A familiar move. Realism is always ideological, and mentalistic realism is the typical ideology of the intellectuals. It needs to be demythologized.

Briefly then, thinking is pictured on the metaphor of seeing, which in turn has always been represented in language as a sort of long-distance palpation. We take the old prescientific optics first. Human eyes have long been spoken of as *lamps* or torches. They may be *bright* or *dim*. They emit directional *beams*, with which we *scan* the environment. Our gaze *sweeps* the horizon, or *travels* around a room until it *lights* upon something of interest to us.

Interestingly, there is a lust of the eyes. When our gaze alights upon something desirable to us, it may become more *sparkling, intense, fiery, burning*[13] or even *devouring*. With our modern scientific theory before us, we are doubtless aware that in such a case all that is happening is that the iris is widening. But the pre-scientific metaphoric, derived from the Bible as well as from the Greeks, continues in language. So we still talk as if vision were a kind of palpation, feeling, *caressing* and even *feasting upon* its object, and as if the power-output of radiant energy from the eyes could be varied.

So much for the metaphoric of vision. Secondly, it was the Greeks in particular who took all this material and re-used it to describe the way the mind's eye apprehends objects in the world of thought.[14] To build on, there was already a long tradition of speaking of secret thoughts, rebellious impulses, unacted intentions and suchlike as being concealed within the heart. There was also talk of inner pictures such as dreams, fantasies and the more vivid memories. So one can already imagine the development of an inner space in which the mind's eye views pictures, and where conflicting inner forces wrestle.

The Greek discovery of theory, logic, the mathematical basis of nature and conceptual analysis led to a very great elaboration of these ideas. The intellect now became a power that reached out to, palpated, apprehended and comprehended purely intelligible objects in an intelligible world. The crucial point is that pure thought is represented as being visionary and supralinguistic, the mind supposedly sharing with the eye the capacity to reach out and grasp its objects. Notice the vocabulary of mental *power*, *grasp*, *grip*, *sharpness*, *acuity*, *force*, *incisiveness* and *comprehension*: although we are still in language, the metaphors are working to create the impression that the mind can function in a region beyond language and can do better than language. Where language is merely secondary, metaphorical and discursive, pure thought, being *contemplative*, *speculative*, *intuitive* and *theoretical* (all of them visual metaphors), is capable of getting a hold of mental objects as they really are.

But we are still in language! All the talk, popular even today, of a world of thought in which the mind wanders around contemplating eternal verities is only a linguistic construct, a myth generated by metaphors of metaphors. Furthermore, the Philosophical Right since even before Plato have had their own motives for projecting out their myths. Their ideology works to entrench and secure the devices by which they flatter themselves and set themselves up as superior to the common people.

As I have shown, I don't believe a word of it. For me language, metaphor and narrative do go all the way down. I don't accept even the hard Philosophical Right's view that there are a lot of pre-cultural and purely objective, but very unpleasant, facts about the human condition, which are non-narrative and just the same for every human being. On the contrary, sickness, old age, suffering, death, transience and futility are construed in very different ways in different religions and philosophies. They do not *first* have a true natural meaning of their own, prior to their incorporation into culture. Rather, they are going to mean to us what we make them mean. They come out having one value or another according to the metaphoric and the rituals with which we invest them. We can make old age venerable or pitiful. We can make death either the crown of life and the achievement of the highest social status, or we can make it an outrage. The choice is ours.

In which case the true democratization of Philosophy is the deconstruction of its pretensions. Capital-P Philosophy only discouraged people by so effectively claiming superior knowledge for so long. While it was around it devalorized the people's way of creating meanings and values by their myths, their art, their rituals and their metaphors. But the modern critique of Philosophy leads us to the realization that there's nothing wrong with the popular religion. Admittedly, it's humanly-evolved, it's just language – but then, what isn't? *What isn't?*

VI

CHANGING THE WORLD

1. The history of the end of history

In the modern West people pose the question about 'the meaning of life' in markedly individualistic terms – and don't get very far with it. They might do better if they rephrased the question in terms of the meaning of history, for that would remind them of an ancient literary tradition, going back to the Hebrew Bible, which sets the question about the individual in the larger context of the destiny of the community. But maybe nowadays people feel forced to ask about the meaning of life, rather than the meaning of history, because in recent years we have somehow lost the ability to speak about the ultimate destiny of large groups such as the nation, the church or the race. If so, that loss is itself an important matter, and needs to be examined.

The question of the meaning of history is a literary question. Our language does not make any clear distinction between history as a train of events and history as a kind of writing, because there isn't any clear distinction between the two things. Events are first formed and produced *as* events only within the language, at first spoken and then later written, in which they are recounted.[1] There is no access to history except through language. History exists only in language. And the developed literary forms in which historical narratives come to be cast always embody theories about the ground, the course and the goal of history – in short, about the meaning of our life.

At the beginning of our religious tradition history was constructed as pretty much a solo performance by God. It was a record of the fulfilment of his purposes, of all the threats and promises he had announced in particular through his prophets. It was the drama of an unfolding divine self-revelation. Yet there was something paradoxical about this, because in the Deuteronomic histories God as himself a character scarcely figures. The stage is occupied entirely by human beings, so that the revelation of God in the story is perforce indirect. Yet it is progressive, at least in the sense that as the nation's historical experience accumulates the story of God's dealings with people grows longer, and so presumably teaches more lessons. It seems natural to conclude that the drama must lead up to and history must end in a complete and immediate self-presencing of God, the Parousia. This final act of self-revelation will also be a Last Judgment, because by fully manifesting his own power and glory God must finally overcome all his enemies and banish evil and ambiguity from the world. It also seems natural to suppose that God's final self-vindicating arrival in person will be most spectacular if it comes at the very moment when it is most desperately needed, because evil is at its most triumphant. This in turn suggests that, so far as the ultimate historical Event is concerned, we will be helpless and God will do everything. In the worst times we human beings can only watch, pray and keep alive the Advent hope.

Thus for many, many centuries God, though off-stage, was in effect the only historical agent. The Parousia was described in various ways. It was the coming of the Son of Man upon the clouds of Heaven. It was the return of Christ in glory to judge the living and the dead, and to establish his millennial kingdom. But as the Christian centuries rolled by the Parousia tended to recede further into the future.[2] Human history began to develop within the interim-period of waiting thereby opened up. At least we human beings could occupy ourselves with building up the church, giving the elect of other nations their chance to hear the gospel, and purifying our own souls so that we should not be unprepared to meet our Maker.

At the beginning of our tradition then, and indeed for over two millennia, God controlled the basic conditions of historical existence and predestined in detail the entire course of world events. The one really important and certain future event was the Parousia. If the universal Parousia and Judgment were deferred, then one still certainly had to face a mini-version of it, in the shape of one's own death and the personal accounting that would follow. Inevitably, Christian ethics was chiefly – and so far as most believers were concerned, almost exclusively – concerned with the self; with personal conversion, purification, sanctification and final salvation. Only as God receded somewhat and the scope for human historical action grew, could Christian ethics relax and begin to look around.

In this enlargement of scope I suggest the main stages are as follows. First, there is the movement from personal ethics to social ethics, as more positive religious value comes to be assigned to 'particular friendships', marriage and other social relationships. Secondly there is the movement from social ethics to issue-politics, as believers campaign to secure legislation on particular topics of great concern to them. Thirdly, there is the movement from issue-politics to a broader political critique, such as one finds in writers like R. H. Tawney and Reinhold Niebuhr. Fourthly, just as philosophy has become more aware of its own historical and cultural context, so religious thought is nowadays becoming more concerned with culture-criticism. This culture-criticism may take the form of communal self-criticism, as when Christians start to question their own tradition's historic preoccupation with power, patriarchy and platonism. Or it may take the form of a critique of contemporary secular culture. Finally there is the movement from culture-criticism to world-criticism, which has hardly yet begun but which the newer anti-realist philosophy clearly calls for. If we make truth and we produce reality, then we ought to be more aware than we are of our own responsibility for our own perceptions of things. Self-criticism and world-criticism imply each other. What you are determines what you see, what you see is very often a kind of judgment upon what you are. As we become more aware of our own language and of the freight of ideology and valuations that it carries, so we become more aware of the interplay between the self that produces language and the world that is produced in and by language.

By this time the Last Judgment has become fully demythologized: it has become a mode of the religious consciousness. It has also become, as we shall see, the basis of a new possibility of history.

Six stages, then, in the development of religious ethics: personal ethics, social ethics, issue-politics, political criticism, culture-criticism and world-criticism. The development from stage to stage reflects changes in the felt character of historical experience and indeed of our moral responsibility. What do I feel responsible for; what do I feel I ought to try to do something about? At first primarily, and almost solely, the salvation of my own soul. But then, very gradually, my immediate social relationships. Then I get the idea that I should band together with others and struggle to secure the removal of some scandalous social evil. Then we address the political set-up under which we live. Next, the inherited cultural construction of reality. Then the environment and our perception of the physical world. Step by step we take control, as the field of our responsibility widens. One thing after another, that used to be regarded as natural and unalterably predetermined by God, comes instead to be seen as having all along been only a human historical construct that we ought to take over and redesign. We began preoccupied with the salvation from the world of our own metaphysical souls. We end with a strange fulfilment-and-reversal of Jesus' teaching: we have lost our souls and have gained the whole world.

Only, it's not a 'real' world any more. We came progressively to assume responsibility for the social order, morality, politics, culture and the environment, only insofar as we came to see that all our established conceptions about these things were just temporary human fictions. The world had to become less real so that it could come to be seen by us as humanly constructed and therefore humanly changeable.

But that same relative 'unreality' infects the human subject also. The human subject as a metaphysical subject, a rational soul more-or-less prior to and independent of history and the body, was already in dire trouble even before Darwin, but in William James and Nietzsche it clearly disappears. With it go unchanging Reason and Truth out-there. The resulting life without nature is not easy. Consider the plight of a radical feminist. She recognizes now that her gender-identity as a woman is a variable cultural fiction, and she rejects the forms in which femininity has been constructed hitherto. But there is no 'natural' womanhood for her to recover. So her position is: 'I am a fiction that I reject, and there is nothing given to tell me how to reinvent myself'. Tough. *But that is the position we are all of us in, about everything!*

In the fully-developed cultural condition which is at present called postmodernism our historical reflection perforce becomes world-critical. Everything is under judgment – including any standards that might have been invoked to guide the work of reconstruction. So we are nihilists, and our model for new-style historical action, without criteria and therefore without progress, becomes artistic creativity. After the universal judgment comes the task of building a new world, unguided.

To get some sort of perspective on where we stand now, we need to form a view about whether the death of Man and the end of history have occurred or not. That in turn requires us to raise the earlier question of the death of God and the coming-of-age of Man. So we need a historical genealogy of the present. Since the present is a condition in which everything is invented, everything is a fiction, *our* fiction, its genealogy must also be fictional; but it still needs to be an illuminating, interesting fiction.

I place the death of God around 1730, at the end of the last generation of realistic metaphysical theists. The chief names are John Locke (1632–1704), G. W. Leibniz (1646–1716), Samuel Clarke (1675–1729), Nicolas Malebranche (1638–1715), George Berkeley (1685–1753) and Christian Wolff (1679–1754). Widely though their philosophies differed, these six were all realistic theists. The use of the word 'God' in their texts is governed by a more-or-less common set of rules. They are clearly all of them referring to and talking about one and the same public Object, established in the public realm outside their respective philosophies, in a way that has not been true of any subsequent generation of major thinkers.

Mind you, they were already somewhat post-Christian. Most of them fell short of positively affirming the orthodox doctrines of the Trinity and the Incarnation. They inclined to Unitarianism, and were very much aware of the difficulty of maintaining an orthodox Christian cosmology in a scientific age. The last fairly-competent attempt to assert a traditional and comprehensive Christian-platonic philosophical theology was made by Ralph Cudworth in *The True Intellectual System of the Universe* (1678). But Cudworth failed. Mechanism defeated platonism, and the six whom I have called the last generation of realistic theists were therefore already slightly deviant, and slightly rearguard in tone.

As for the key social events of 1660–1710 or so, we should point not only to such textbook examples as the triumphs of the new science, the Glorious Revolution, religious toleration and free trade, but still more to vast engineering projects successfully executed, such as the draining of the Fens[3] and the rebuilding of London. Other things that could be mentioned include the increasing collection of government statistics, the emergence of secular historiography, the consciousness that the Moderns had now surpassed the Ancients, the belief therefore in Progress, 'the spirit of improvement' with its determined efforts to measure and achieve control of time and space, and the concept of the social contract, important as an attempt to demystify the origins of society and political authority.

Out of all these things emerges 'Man', in the strong sense: a fully Enlightened, autonomous historical subject who sets out to rationalize society, control nature and take charge of the future, a human subject who develops and applies objectively-valid scientific knowledge and rational principles so as progressively to optimize the condition of human beings in the world.

'Man' in that sense flourished in the eighteenth and nineteenth centuries. For 'Man', there was still a cosmos out there and Truth out there. Human nature – and therefore human well-being, and therefore the moral standard – was a given constant. There were therefore norms independent of history by which historical progress could be guided and assessed, and this made it possible for the old eschatological history to continue in new half-secularized forms. The agent guiding history towards its future consummation was admittedly now not God, but 'Man'. But the change of steersman had some advantages. It made for simplicity, for instead of the old two-level 'man-proposes-but-God-disposes' type of writing, history could now be written as a one-level story of human actions. Its goal was now immanent – that is, it could be clearly envisaged as brought into being by us on earth. It was not something supernatural that could only be vaguely imagined and passively awaited: it was going to be the direct historical outcome of our own present endeavours. It was the anarchist Utopia, it was the Kingdom of God on earth, it was the communist society, it was the New Jerusalem, it was the Kingdom of Ends, it was a fully *transparent* world,[4] rationalized and reconciled. The struggles of the masses got 'meaning', in the sense of instrumental value, insofar as they really could be seen as contributing to the realization of a better world in the future.

For all this to be believable three main groups of conditions must be fulfilled. History has to be progressive and progressing; history has to be totalizable and getting totalized; and history has to have what I shall call a frame.

The first of these groups of conditions has to do with progress. As we have said earlier, there has to be some generally-recognized yardstick independent of history by which historical progress can be measured, and there has to be an accepted way of applying the yardstick to present conditions and so demonstrating to the general satisfaction that a measurable advance is being made. This leads us directly to the second group of conditions, which have to do with totalization. Much of human life is lived at cross purposes. The progress-yardstick cannot be applied unless my labours and those of my enemy can be synthesized in some larger whole in which both of us can find fulfilment. In fact the progress-yardstick cannot be applied unless a world-historical dialectic is at work everywhere, mediating and synthesizing, unifying history and making it make overall sense. In short, we have to think of world-history taken all together as both totalizable and actually getting totalized. And this leads to the question of framework-conditions. For the grand historicist Hegel-to-Toynbee picture we are now conjuring up calls on us to view the whole of world history as one vast story, unfolding step by predestined step within a single ordered space-time framework. Within this framework, the Meaning of it All is realized in a manner that is public, universal and True for peoples of all ages and cultures.

In short, historicism is riven by an inner contradiction. It begins by claiming to be post-metaphysical, but inevitably ends up highly metaphysical after all. It begins by promising *both* to do justice to the variety of historical periods, cultures and human endeavours *and* to tell its story in such a way as to show how the struggles of ordinary suffering humanity contribute to the march of Spirit. But if it is to have a yardstick, if it is to totalize history, and if it is to think the cosmological setting within which the historical progress unfolds, then it cannot help but get metaphysical again. To put the point at its simplest, the Telos or Goal of history must itself become an ultimate and history-transcending Standard of Truth and Value out there, by which everything else is judged.

In the heyday of theology, history got unified because one powerful and all-wise God planned and controlled it all. In the age of 'Man' history was the product of the struggles and conflicts of billions of people, speaking thousands of different languages. To unify Man-made history, the thinker must postulate a number of hidden agencies at work joining things up, and also some history-transcending criterion for recognizing that the history-ending, history-transcending goal of history has been reached. Thus, in the communist society human nature, the human *Gattungswesen* as it really is, is really fulfilled – and everything has become theological again. The strong capitalized doctrine of Man as the godlike Maker of his own history still requires a transcendent unification, at least in an unchanging human essence, above history and then getting realized within history. But this essence-doctrine would be very seriously threatened by any really deep sense of historical or cultural relativity. Once people start to think that there's no such thing as a human 'nature' quite independent of historical and cultural change, then obviously Man with a capital M is in trouble, and totalized world-history is in trouble.

Humanist-eschatological history was therefore bound to fail. It needs to claim a little bit of transcendence on behalf of its yardstick of progress, its theory of totalization, its doctrine of human nature, its conception of a final human fulfilment and so on; but all ideas about these things are themselves local historical products that quickly date. Everyone has noticed how science-fiction visions of the future very quickly become outdated and cease to tell us anything about the future. Instead, they come to speak more and more revealingly about the period when they were written. The rule is that what today purports to be transcendent, will tomorrow be seen to have been merely immanent after all.

The humanist-eschatological conception of history typical of the Modern period was violently attacked by Nietzsche, though it lingered on in Europe until 1968. The events in Paris in May of that year suggested to a whole generation of the French that Man was dead – meaning, that under late capitalism in the most advanced countries the state is so powerful and consumerism so seductive that the working class will never again take to the streets and seize the reins of history. Further, the individual human being is dead too, because Durkheim and Saussure have respectively demonstrated that society and language radically precede the individual. So Man is dead, in the sense that the vast administrative, economic and cultural machine of the modern State is no longer under Enlightened control, and cannot again be brought under such control. Perhaps Lenin is to blame for all this. He slew Man and humanist eschatology, by founding the modern out-of-control totalitarian State that has now discredited socialism. In this climate of pessimism deconstruction is a last resort, an attempt to destabilize a little the totalitarian sign-system that holds us captive. But Man is dead.[5] And the analysis suggests that the death of Man coincides with the end of the idea that history has a great and blessed End.

Then came 1989, the year of miracles, when the common people, simply by turning out on the streets in sufficient numbers and with sufficient determination and persistence in the cold Autumn weather, blew away half-a-dozen seemingly impregnable totalitarian governments. They did not for the most part initiate violence, and they were not led by professional revolutionary groups. In fact their popular revolutions were protests against ideology, against the communist party, and especially against Leninism and the leading role of the party in the totalitarian state. Artists, writers and students were conspicuous among the early leaders. These people were sick of grandiose schemes for human redemption proclaimed in ugly inflated language, which promised everything but delivered only repression. They had no political nostrums of their own. They just wanted ordinary low-key humanity: human rights and freedom of expression. They repudiated decisively what I have been calling the humanist-eschatological conception of history. Their revolt was a revolt of people against Man. There must be no more rhetoric, no more grand designs.

1989, then, has a dual meaning. On the one hand it was a popular revolution against Revolution. It was a refusal any longer to be deceived. It was a second atheism, the slaying of Man, the end of messianic revolutionary humanism. On the other hand, this death of Man appears as a most joyful sacrifice, and a rebirth for ordinary, sceptical low-key human beings. Nihilism means the death of God followed by the death of Man; it means the end of metaphysics followed by the end of ideology. *And nihilism is also a humanism!* History with a capital H, the big machine going somewhere, we'll do without. We will not believe in anything that claims absoluteness, closure or finality. We will limit our trust to what is ambiguous and endless – human relationships, the imagination, artistic creativity, and the symbolism (*only* the symbolism) of religion.

2. World-production, world-transformation

Many people think of the world as being simply there, inertly factual and independent of us. Not so: since our minds, *as* minds, work only in language, nothing is real and nothing is there until it has been formed and produced in and by language. And in fact the notion that the world is self-existent has been uncommon in our tradition. It has been much more usual to attribute the world's existence to some kind of productive language-using agency. Its speech forms the world. Religion calls this agency God. Critical thinking calls it religion, observing that in all cultures religion seems originally to have supplied the vocabulary in terms of which the world-order, human selfhood, time, evil and human destiny are symbolized.

So the world is made, poetically, by God, and a little more prosaically, by religious language. However, religious world-building is communal and largely unconscious. So there has also been the attempt by philosophy, both in Greek antiquity and in early modern Europe, to demythologize the whole business of world-production. A book of philosophy conjures up a vision of the world, characterizes it, lays it out before us, gives us an account of our own place within it and, above all, shows where the levers are; that is, it shows us at what points and in what ways we can intervene most effectively. All this with a view to suggesting a form of practice, a way of so relating ourselves to the world that we can transform it and thereby transform also ourselves. (Notice that there is not much point in changing the one unless we can at the same time also change the other. The world is the other-than-us: changing it we change ourselves, and changing ourselves we change it.) At any rate, in the modern philosophy which began with Descartes the practical interest is always present. And our entire discussion has suggested a broad contrast between the way the Enlightenment, following Descartes, has constructed and still constructs the world, and an alternative art-and-language vision of the world which is both older and newer.

Let us be brutally schematic about this. We have three visions of the world to compare, classical, modern and postmodern. They are related as thesis, antithesis and synthesis. In the classical vision the world was God's work of art, produced by God's almighty Word. In the modern vision the world was constructed as a machine operating in accordance with general mathematical rules, a machine of whose workings we might gain complete understanding and control. In the postmodern vision the world is represented as our expression, our fiction, our communally-produced and ever-changing work of art. We need a new kind of religion for this new world, an objectless, abstract practice of life as expressive religious art.

First, the thesis. Classical philosophy before 1600 had a predominantly contemplative emphasis. So did classical religion. There was widespread acceptance of the primacy of the contemplative life. God had produced the world by language as his own self-expression and so that it might be the theatre of his own action. In short, God was a romantic artist and an idealist philosopher. The Ideas in his mind had formed the created order that he beheld, so that God was like the epistemological subject in Kant's philosophy. He knew the world inside out because every last detail of it had got its shape precisely from his own formative understanding of it. By knowing he created, by creating he knew. As Kant sapiently remarks, 'reason has insight only into that which it produces after a plan of its own'.[6] Reason legislates. What God had made by his lawgiving Word, he had formed in every part: he therefore understood it completely and had complete control over it.

Hence the primacy of contemplation: God had done everything perfectly already. In the human realm there are a very few potters, painters and other craftspeople who towards the close of their careers achieve a technical mastery over their medium so consummate that it seems almost casual and playful, like the finest Japanese calligraphy. Even today, that quality strikes us as being something worshipful. Indeed, it may be the most religious thing we have left. Certainly in the heyday of theology God was seen as having just that quality. At the close of the very first elaborated Christian narrative of the entire Plan of Salvation the apostle exclaims, 'O the depth of the riches and wisdom and knowledge of God! How unsearchable are his judgments and how inscrutable his ways!'[7] A theology might even be defined as a piece of writing designed to provoke just such a response of awe and wonder. We contemplate the whole story of God's world-production and world-mastery, the ways in which he bends and turns the narrative so as to achieve the final salvation of mankind and the fulfilment of all his purposes, and we are enraptured.

In classical Christianity the believer thus adored God's world-mastery and was its beneficiary. You felt yourself to be upborne by God's providence and his Grace. But the authorized forms of words very severely limited the extent to which you could participate in and exercise something of God's perfect world-control. The New Testament itself is fairly relaxed about these matters, and is willing to speak of believers as having 'tasted the goodness of the word of God and the powers of the age to come',[8] as being called to 'work out your own salvation',[9] and so on – language which seems to give the believer an active role. But in later theology, Pelagianism and 'synergism'[10] were widely regarded as heretical. A fundamentally sexist metaphoric dominated the orthodox accounts of the relation of God to the soul, relegating the believer to an ultra-feminine secondariness and subordination. You could never take the initiative. You must always wait for your Lord to make the first move. You could never devise any good work except under his guidance, nor accomplish it without the help of his enabling grace. Inhibited by this crushing theological sexism, classical Christianity could never fully realize its programme of human emancipation. Standard forms of words appeared to require that the believer must never dream of being anything more than a dutiful and submissive wife, utterly content to bear her husband's name and to be a channel for the expression of his power and glory, without any aspiration to become anything on her own account.

So in classical Christianity, both Catholic and Reformed, God's supreme power and mastery framed and controlled every part of the world and every detail of its history in a way that prompted the believer to an ecstatic and joyful response of worship and thanksgiving. But the approved linguistic forms – and it needs to be stressed that in classical Christianity language was indeed very tightly policed – the approved linguistic forms, I say, ascribed everything to God and almost nothing to the human being. The believer aimed to be superwife, irreproachably discreet, self-negating and invisible. The human agent did not seek any autonomous world-control or world-mastery, and even co-operation with God sounded a little too presumptuous. And this religious vocabulary inevitably discouraged scientific research and the development of new technologies. To repeat an example mentioned earlier, nothing was done about the draining of the Fens between the Romans and the seventeenth century, although the same period was one of uninhibitedly sublime artistic achievement. For example: the sculpture at Reims. So classical Christian culture appears to have repressed one sort of human creativity, but not another.

So much for the thesis, the production and control of the world by the divine Word of God. For the antithesis, consider now the entirely different way in which the world is produced in the Enlightenment thought that stems from Descartes and has generated our own science-based industrial culture.

For reasons of discretion, early Enlightenment thought tended to veil its own revolutionary character. But from Descartes onwards, and at least in the sphere of natural philosophy, there is an unmistakable attempt to replace God by Man, art by technology and language by applied mathematics. The world is to be constructed outwards from the human subject, rather than downwards from God. To make all this even remotely plausible, it is necessary to claim that the human subject is rather like God and can become more so, and that it can attain a knowledge of the world and a control over it that are comparable with God's. Descartes' rationalism seems at times to verge on idealism, as if the natural philosopher's Reason legislated *a priori*, giving Nature the orders. And if in the end Descartes does not quite go so far as that, nevertheless he does insist that the human being is the human mind, that the human mind is unsleeping like God because it always thinks, that it is made in God's image and is as much a spiritual thing as God is, and that it understands necessary truth as clearly and distinctly as God does. By an odd and significant error in his logic Descartes infers from 'the proposition "I exist" is necessarily true whenever I entertain it', the very different and startling conclusion that the 'I' itself 'now necessarily exists'.[11] He adds that the 'I' has a will 'that is both extremely ample and also perfect of its kind'.[12] After all this, we are not in the least surprised to read that

> ... I am now experiencing a gradual increase in my knowledge, and I see nothing to prevent its increasing more and more to infinity. Further, I see no reason why I should not be able to use this increased knowledge to acquire all the other perfections of God.[13]

All the evidence is that Descartes tried very hard to produce a text that was theologically unexceptionable. All the more significant, therefore, is the fact that it contains several revealing slips.

Now, it had been an axiom of European thought since antiquity that the human mind is not capable of God's immediate, intuitive and absolute knowledge of everything in all its particularity and just as it is. The human mind is discursive, and understands only through general concepts. If therefore Descartes and the Enlightenment were plausibly to claim that the human mind can in principle know the objective world as clearly and completely as God knows it, then the world had to have only human-mind-type properties. It had to be transparent to the mind of the mathematical physicist. It had to be stripped of all its singularities, its opacities, its complexities. It had to have only general and measurable 'primary' properties.[14] Matter had to be only geometrical, and all changes in the world had to be reducible to mathematically-analysable local motions of geometrical matter.

I am suggesting, then, that Descartes' texts are a takeover bid. They set out to fiction a world of which it can plausibly be claimed that the human subject can know it as clearly as God does. Descartes claims to be close to achieving a complete fundamental science of nature. He gave our science-based industrial culture its barren but necessary vision of the world as being nothing but that to which our applied mathematics applies, and which our engineers can engineer. Descartes in his texts fabricated the world that industrial civilization was going to need, the world with which we are now cursed, the world of which so many scientists are still claiming to have something approaching a complete understanding.

Immensely powerful and influential though it immediately was and has remained ever since, Descartes' vision of the world has two things wrong with it from the outset. Despite his protestations to the contrary, it was a world so drastically reduced as to leave no room for morality, religion or art as they had traditionally been practised. Inevitably after Descartes, a fissure developed in the culture between the view of the world presupposed by scientists and engineers (that is, the physical world is such that in principle a complete description of it can be given in the language of applied mathematics), and the view of the world presupposed by the practice of art, morality and religion. Despite everyone's urgent denials the fissure is still there, as disastrous as ever.

Descartes' second problem arises out of his attempt to solve the first. By mind-body dualism Descartes and many of his successors hoped to reserve a non-physical, 'mental' or 'spiritual' realm within which human thinking could go on and moral, artistic and religious values could be retained. However, the human being is a bodily being, part of the physical world, and what people call the human 'mind' is merely a certain cultural patterning of such bodily performances as working and talking. The human 'mind' is therefore just as much open to analysis by the methods of applied mathematics as any other pattern of physical events. If the weather is a machine and if my dog is a machine, then so am I. Pursuing engineering efficiency, Taylorism[15] analysed industrial labour, breaking it down to a sequence of simple performances, and eventually replacing assembly-line workers by robots. Charles Babbage and George Boole did just the same job for human intellectual tasks, opening the way to the replacement of the human calculator by a machine. Thus applied mathematics demystifies both crafts and intelligence.[16] It de-skills first the manual worker and then the office worker. Nor does the computer revolution exempt the very people who are bringing it about. It moves so fast that, at least in the lower echelons, it makes redundant its own workers too.

The bitter irony of all this is that the Cartesian-Enlightenment dream of humanly-constructed godlike knowledge has led only to the drastic recent secularization and commodification of knowledge; and the Cartesian-Enlightenment dream of total human understanding and control has led to the economic system's total understanding and control of the human being. Cartesianism brought about the death of God in less than one century and the death of Man in less than three.

The thesis then is that in the classical world-view an infinite God creates the Cosmos as a theatre for the display of his own infinite power, glory and goodness. The vision is magnificent, and good for art and religion. But it is bad for science and technology, and makes human beings too radically secondary.

The antithesis sees the modern (or Cartesian-Enlightenment) world-view as the product of a revolt against God. Descartes invented an applied mathematician's universe that could be completely understood by human science, and therefore controlled by human technology. It has split the culture and devoured the human subject. When did you last hear words like soul and conscience used seriously in everyday speech? To say that 'Man is dead' is merely to say that such words are fading out of ordinary language. Thus the modern world view, intended to liberate humanity, has had rather the opposite effect.

The synthesis is a centreless and postmodern vision of the world which has given up the concept of substance. The classical God-centred vision and the modern Man-centred vision both sought to unify the world by focussing it around a Centre, conceived in each case as a centre of understanding, power, control and self-affirmation. But precisely that wish to see the world fully understood and controlled by a self-affirming Ego is what we ought to give up. It is a sexist dream of mastery: nature as a fantasy-woman, completely subservient, responsive to one's slightest desire, and above all, *no problem*. And I am suggesting that these dreams of mastery are vulgar. They are bad art, too self-indulgent. We should give up our received ideas of substance, identity and sovereignty. Instead we should take up again a very beautiful and fascinating theme from ancient mythology, that of the metamorphoses,[17] whereby the identities of humans, gods, animals and plants are endlessly transformed into each other and flow in and out of each other. I am saying that our life-practice needs to be freed from the old sexist-political ideal of a strong Ego, omnipotent power, fixed boundaries and total control. Instead we should see life in more 'aestheticist' terms, as a kind of performance-art. As language shifts, flows and changes all the time, so it carries our own identity and that of everything else with it. Everything undergoes continual reinvention and transformation. We don't hold on; we are mobile, wanderers. We don't have a fixed identity ourselves, and we don't attribute one to anything else. Rather, we float along with language, reimagining and recreating ourselves and our world all the time. We cannot change language much, but we can bend it a little; and even a small rearrangement can make a great difference.

Religious thought hitherto has very often been defensive, authoritarian and fetishistic. Its ideal of mastery has been sexist and imperialistic. We can sense the metaphorical affinity between religious precisionism, engineering precision, and the desire to make the other into a slave over whom we have total control. In each case there is something obsessive, ritualistic and insatiable. I am suggesting that in the practice of life we should pursue a different ideal of mastery, like water in its capacity to take on many shapes, like escapology in its love of slipping away, and like art in its capacity to revalue life by imaginatively transforming it.

CREATION OUT OF NOTHING

Let us pursue by stages the idea of the practice of life as a kind of abstract religious performance-art. First, religion becomes better and more beautiful when the passage of time and a certain cognitive distancing have made it abstract. In North-West Europe there are many hundreds of prehistoric earthworks, standing stones and the like. The original rites and beliefs associated with these places are now lost forever, and they are all the better for it. They have become abstractly sacred, and therefore good religion for today. Being blank, void and aniconic, a stone circle is now sacred in a non-oppressive and imaginatively liberating way.

For an example of the way such an abstract sacred might be built into a way of life, consider secondly the work of the foremost landscape artist of the day, Richard Long.[18] Long is a performance artist at least to the extent that the way he lives is an essential part of his message as an artist, and he does not quite make portable commodity-sculptures. He is a walker, who has traversed much of the world during the past twenty years. He walks alone, backpacking over mountains and deserts. His primary works are the walks themselves and certain traces that he leaves as he goes: arrangements of stones, patterns scraped with the heel of his boot. They are very simply geometrical: a filled-in circular stone pavement, a straight path from which the stones have been cleared, a spiral. Seen in the landscape from a distance they do have a certain monumental and sacred quality. Yet nothing has been added to the landscape. All that has happened is that a few things have been moved around. The work is unmarked, and may or may not be left to survive if it can. Some works have been made by throwing water; others Long himself dismantles before moving on. He says he likes the idea of impermanence. Gallery pieces by Long are constructed in the same spirit. He arranges sticks, stones, words and mud in the simplest geometrical shapes.

One might compare one of Long's works with one of his own footprints. A footprint is a minimal work, a negative work, a mere indentation on the ground, a present absence that betokens a former presence, a human trace. A footprint is several times over a symbol of transience (Latin, going by), for a person did go by, our life is a journey, and as time passes, everything passes away, including this footprint itself. Yet – as Long's works say, and as the prehistoric works he admires also say – there can be something sacred about the trace we leave upon the world. Especially as it wears away. Long is not at all like the type of Renaissance or bourgeois artist whose works are attempts to objectify and immortalize his own subjectivity. On the contrary, the spirit of his work resembles that of high Modernism in its formalism and austerity. The work gets its sacred quality from its impersonality and rigorous dedication to landscape.

So Long walks, but he's not going to any one place in particular. He leaves traces, but they do not express any historically-conditioned human subjectivity. They could have originated either from before history or after it. They may or may not endure. But they do have a sacred quality. And without wishing to over-interpret an important artist, I am suggesting that Long's journeys and his work may be read as symbolizing the continuing possibility of a dedicated and creative religious life, even today.

The demands of our present situation are severe. To break through to something like a truthful religious life we have to pass through nihilism. We must give up entirely certain popular and cherished ideas of God, the self and life's purpose. Instead, there is for us only the realm of signs, within which our changing ideas of the self and the world are produced. But pessimism is a sin, a waste of time. If we are sufficiently disciplined in selflessness we can rearrange things a little and perhaps thereby transform a bit of the world and revalue it. If it is disciplined and impersonal enough, the trace we leave may take on a certain sacred quality. As it fades.

In the past, people who recognized all these hard facts said, 'Yes: and that is what it is to have to do with an invisible God.' Yes.

Notes

I Creating the World out of Nothing

1. In the New Testament, see John 9.6.

2. E.g., Leviticus 20.22, Revelation 3.16.

3. For this and what follows, see J. M. Plumley, 'The Cosmology of Ancient Egypt' in Carmen Blacker and Michael Loewe, *Ancient Cosmologies*, Allen and Unwin 1975, p. 29 and passim.

4. A good sample of Creation myths is presented by Mircea Eliade, *From Primitives to Zen*, Collins 1979, ch. II.

5. Plumley, op. cit., p. 34.

6. Ibid., p. 35.

7. B. Malinowski, *Magic, Science and Religion and Other Essays*, Souvenir Press 1974; Edmund Leach, 'Anthropological approaches to the study of the Bible during the twentieth century'; reprinted in Leach and D. Alan Aycock, *Structuralist Interpretations of Biblical Myth*, Cambridge University Press 1983, pp. 7–32.

8. D. D. Evans, *The Logic of Self-Involvement*, SCM Press 1963.

9. David McLellan (ed.), *Karl Marx: Selected Writings*, Cambridge University Press 1977, p. 94.

10. Ibid., p. 95.

11. Shlomo Avineri, *The Social and Political Thought of Karl Marx*, Cambridge University Press 1968, pp. 65–77, has a good summary. See p. 69: 'Marx's epistemology occupies a middle position between classical materialism and classical idealism . . . since it synthesizes the two traditions, it transcends the classic dichotomy between subject and object. Indirectly this synthesis solves the Kantian antinomy between the cognitive and the moral spheres.'

12. For a short defence of the slogan, 'Transcendental idealism, empirical realism', see Kant's *Critique of Pure Reason*, A336–380.

13. Cited from Arthur C. Danto, *Nietzsche as Philosopher*, Columbia University Press 1980 edition, p. 76.

14. Jacques Lacan, *Écrits I*, Seuil 1966, p. 155.

15. For interpretations of the early Derrida see Rodolphe Gasché, *The Tain of the Mirror*, Harvard 1986; Eve Tavor Bannett, *Structuralism and the Logic of Dissent*, Macmillan 1989; and Richard Rorty, *Contingency, Irony and Solidarity*, Cambridge University Press 1989.

16. From *For a Critique of the Political Economy of the Sign*, St Louis: Telos Press 1981, p. 155; cited by Richard Harland, *Superstructuralism*, Methuen 1987.

17. Stephen Houlgate, *Hegel, Nietzsche and the Criticism of Metaphysics*, Cambridge University Press 1986, argues that Hegel is more consistently and satisfactorily post-metaphysical than even Nietzsche.

NOTES

18. Rorty, *Contingency, Irony and Solidarity*, Cambridge 1989.

19. Compare Leszek Kolakowski, *Metaphysical Horror*, Blackwell 1988, p. 52, on the way 'the contemporary philosophical divinization of language' might make it possible for 'God and the Absolute to reassert their legal presence in our tongue.' Are we then here trying to do exactly what Rorty and (ambiguously) Kolakowski warn against? Not quite, as I hope will be apparent.

II Nihilism

1. David Hume, *A Treatise of Human Nature*, I, IV, 1. For a short account of the literary background to Montaigne's popularization of scepticism, see Peter Burke, *Montaigne*, Oxford University Press 1981, ch. 3. To the short bibliography on Burke's p. 76, add R. H. Popkin, 'David Hume: His Pyrrhonism and His Critique of Pyrrhonism'; in V. C. Chappell (ed.), *Hume*, Macmillan 1966.

2. L. Wittgenstein, *On Certainty*, Blackwell 1969, is the outstanding case of a philosopher who does not try to answer scepticism with certainty, but instead seeks to undermine and disarm it.

3. W. Von Leyden, *Seventeenth Century Metaphysics*, Duckworth 1968; Edward Craig, *The Mind of God and the Works of Man*, Cambridge University Press 1987.

4. Orthodox Reformed Protestantism and Conservative Evangelicalism strive instinctively for objectivism or realism in their view of religious truth. During the nineteenth century the Anglo-American kind of Evangelical Protestantism allied itself with the Scottish 'philosophy of common sense' precisely because Thomas Reid and his followers were so realistic, and it has remained so allied. Protestant commonsense realism has the merit of a certain robust thisworldliness, but also shares with many forms of Catholic realism an ugly, ungodly preoccupation with certainty, legitimacy and power.

5. For *The Will to Power*, see the Walter Kaufmann edition, New York: Vintage Press 1968.

6. See Hilary Lawson and Lisa Appignanesi (eds.), *Dismantling Truth: Reality in the Post-Modern World*, Weidenfeld and Nicholson 1989.

7. On this, see J.-F. Lyotard's *Le Différend*, 1984, of which an English translation has recently been published (Manchester University Press 1989).

8. Louis Althusser, 'Freud and Lacan', in *Lenin and Philosophy and Other Essays*, New Left Books 1971.

9. Notebook A, 429; in A. A. Luce and T. E. Jessop (eds.), *The Works of George Berkeley*, Volume 1, Nelson 1948, p. 53.

10. Hilary Putnam (*Reason, Truth and History*, Cambridge University Press 1981, ch. 1) has argued that the brains-in-a-vat hypothesis is self-refuting because you have to presuppose realism in order to state it. But Berkeley is better off, for he is a realist about God and he doesn't doubt that our sense-data are truly given and veridical. So Berkeley can fairly insist that 'We see the Horse it self' (A 427) and has no difficulty in referring to the horse, whereas the

NOTES

brain-in-a-vat would never really see a horse and could never genuinely succeed in referring to one.

11. John A. T. Robinson, *Where Three Ways Meet*, SCM Press 1987, pp. 182ff.

12. Ibid., p. 186.

13. Nietzsche, *Twilight of the Idols*, 'The Four Great Errors', 8.

14. James Gleick, *Chaos*, Penguin: Sphere Books 1987.

15. Bernard Williams, *Ethics and the Limits of Philosophy*, Collins Fontana 1985, p. 33.

16. My account here is obviously indebted to Julian Jaynes, *The Origin of Consciousness in the Breakdown of the Bicameral Mind*, Allen Lane 1979. On which see an excellent article by D. C. Stove, 'The Oracles and Their Cessation: A Tribute to Julian Jaynes'; *Encounter*, April 1989. But Jaynes to my mind is too psychologistic. How can one usefully ascribe mental states of one kind or another to people who lived thousands of years ago? So I have turned Jaynes' ideas in a rather more linguistic direction, and might have done so in a much more thoroughgoing way. The key to the whole Bible is its nostalgia for speech and its odd, paradoxical attempt to blur the distinction between speech and writing.

17. See in this connection the recent work on language of Donald Davidson.

18. S. T. Coleridge, *Confessions of An Inquiring Spirit*, 1840 is an exceptionally interesting text to read in the light of the paradoxes here pointed out.

19. William James, *Pragmatism* and *The Meaning of Truth*, Harvard 1978, p. 85.

20. Ibid., p. 87.

21. See John Forrester, 'Lying on the Couch'; in Lawson and Appignanesi, cited above, n. 6.

III The Turning

1. Hence the title of D. F. Pears' fine study of Wittgenstein's thought, *The False Prison*, 2 vols., Oxford University Press 1987, 1988. And see my *The Leap of Reason*, reprinted SCM Press 1985, pp. 31–7; and *Life Lines*, SCM Press 1986, p. 158.

2. Eg., Elizabeth Haldane and G. R. T. Ross, *The Philosophical Works of Descartes*, Cambridge University Press 1969, Vol. I, p. 167.

3. *Where Three Ways Meet* (cited in Part Two, n. 11), p. 186.

4. John A. T. Robinson, *Wrestling with Romans*, SCM Press 1979, p. 19.

5. C. H. Dodd, *The Bible and the Greeks*, Hodder and Stoughton 1935, pp. 82–95.

6. I developed the Cambridge doctrine a stage further in my *Taking Leave of God*, SCM Press 1980, esp. pp. 92ff., a passage clearly also influenced by Kierkegaard's great discourse on 'The Unchangeableless of God' (see *Kierkegaard's Writings*, Princeton edn. Vol. XXIII, 1987).

NOTES

7. For the names of these liberals, see the authors of A. R. Vidler (ed.) *Soundings*, Cambridge University Press 1962. Add the names of John Hick, Maurice Wiles, Arthur Peacocke, John Robinson, etc.

8. Best met by R. B. Braithwaite, 'An Empiricist's View of the Nature of Religious Belief', Cambridge University Press 1955.

9. Freud's phrase is 'the plasticity and free mobility of the libido'; *New Introductory Lectures* (trans. Ernest Jones, 1922), p. 290. For the 'adhesiveness' of libido, see p. 292. But I do not think Freud recognized what has become a commonplace of advanced consumer societies, that the whole cultural-economic system now depends upon lifelong free mobility of libido, and its 'adhesion' therefore to a long succession of different symbolic forms fabricated and presented to it by culture.

10. Jung postulates in the psyche a set of innate propensities towards certain forms for libido to flow into. These are the celebrated 'archetypes'. They are the outcome of his search for cross-cultural universals and his attempt, when he thought he had found them, to build them into a universal human nature. But this is mythical thinking: the archetypes are forms or signs, and therefore simply cultural.

11. Peter F. Anson, *Fashions in Church Furnishings 1840–1940*, 2nd edition, Studio Vista 1965, is an entertaining demonstration of the point. The author cheerfully incorporates ladies in fashionable dress of the period into his own drawings of the East ends of smart churches.

12. *The Existence of God*, Oxford University Press 1979, p. 254.

13. Ibid.

14. Ibid., p. 268.

15. J.-F. Lyotard, *The Postmodern Condition: A Report on Knowledge*, Minnesota/Manchester Universities 1984.

IV   A Theory of God

1. See Michael J. Buckley S.J., *At the Origins of Modern Atheism*, Yale University Press 1987, for a good historical survey.

2. E.g., James Collins, *God in Modern Philosophy*, Chicago: Henry Regnery Co. 1959.

3. In particular, Wilhelm Schmidt, *Der Ursprung der Gottesidee*, 1912 etc. See Eric J. Sharpe, *Comparative Religion: A History*, Duckworth 1975, pp. 182–4.

4. E. E. Evans-Pritchard, *Theories of Primitive Religion*, Oxford University Press 1975; John Skorupski, *Symbol and Theory: A Philosophical Study of Theories of Religion in Social Anthropology*, Cambridge University Press 1976.

5. William J. Hynes and William Dean (eds.), *American Religious Empiricism: Working Papers: Vol. 1*, Regis College Press 1988; Nancy Frankenberry, *Religion and Radical Empiricism*, State University of New York Press 1987.

NOTES

6. For warrior-gods see, for example, Georges Dumézil's works on the pantheons of Indo-European societies. E.g. *L'Iéologie tripartie des Indo-Européens*, Brussels 1958.

7. All this is said very well by John D. Caputo, 'Mysticism and Transgression: Derrida and Meister Eckhart'; in Hugh J. Silverman (ed.), *Continental Philosophy II: Derrida and Deconstruction*, Routledge 1989. See especially pp. 29ff.

8. Again I am indebted to Julian Jaynes, cited above, II, n. 16. But my interpretation ends up being very different from his.

9. The *Phaedrus*, and Jeremiah 31.33. Jeremiah has the same oddity that Derrida makes so much of in Plato. Writing on the heart is supposed to be that much more real and potent and close and unmistakable than exterior writing. But how can it be, when it is still *writing*?

10. Exodus 3.14.

11. Very good on all this is Jean-Jacques Lecercle, *Philosophy Through the Looking-Glass*, Hutchinson (Problems of Modern European Thought Series) 1985.

12. For a more detailed (and slightly different) analysis, see my *The Long-Legged Fly*, SCM Press 1987. That book too contains only metaphors. There *isn't* anything else.

13. Jeremiah 20.9.

14. As a writer himself, though, Paul gets as close as he can to saying flatly that glossolalia is unacceptable: see the lengthy, troubled discussion in I Corinthians 14.

15. Throughout this section my chief debt is of course to Jacques Derrida, and especially to his *Writing and Difference* and *Of Grammatology*, both of which first appeared in 1967. But see also, for example, Jack Goody, *The Domestication of the Savage Mind*, Cambridge University Press 1977, and the work by Julian Jaynes which has been cited above.

16. Jeremiah 36.

17. Ibid., vv. 23, 32.

18. I Kings 21.20.

19. See the Council of Trent on Scripture and Tradition, Session IV, 8 April 1546.

20. Along these lines the Death of God theology can be seen as a radicalization of the doctrine of the Incarnation. To communicate himself to us God must put himself into human words, and so suffer what Roland Barthes in a famous essay called 'The Death of the Author': *Image-Music-Text*, Fontana Paperbacks, Flamingo series 1977. See also the excellent discussion of Thomas J. J. Altizer's recent work in Mark C. Taylor, *Tears*, State University of New York Press 1990, especially ch. 5.

21. *The World as Will and Representation*, 2nd edition 1844, Supplementary chapter XIX; *Parerga and Paralipomena* §118 etc.

22. A point well-made by Richard Rorty in his comments on the early work

of Derrida: *Contingency, Irony and Solidarity*, Cambridge University Press 1989, pp. 122ff.

23. See my *The New Christian Ethics*, SCM Press 1988, passim.

V   Language and the Self

1. In *Contingency, Irony and Solidarity* (cited above, IV, n. 22), p. 73ff.

2. Emanuel Swedenborg, *The True Christian Religion* (1771), Everyman's Library edition, J. M. Dent 1933, p. 28.

3. For the case the other way, see for example Colin McGinn, *The Character of Mind*, Oxford University Press 1982, ch. 4.

4. E.g., Mark 2.6–8.

5. On this see John Cottingham, *Descartes*, Blackwell 1986, p. 45 at n. 31. Cottingham quotes evidence that Descartes indeed held the traditional view, going back to Aristotle, that 'linguistic terms are merely the outward clothing of inner thoughts which are directly manifest to the thinker' (p. 46).

6. On extreme spatial and temporal compression as key features of postmodernity see David Harvey, *The Condition of Postmodernity*, Blackwell 1989.

7. Amos 5.18–20.

8. John R. Hinnells, *Persian Mythology*, Hamlyn 1973, esp. pp. 60–73.

9. Hugh J. Silverman (ed.), *Continental Philosophy I: Philosophy and Non-Philosophy since Merleau-Ponty*, Routledge 1988.

10. This is the common element in the teaching about religion of William James and Ludwig Wittgenstein.

11. See the review-article by Stephen Homes of Leo Strauss, *The Birth of Classical Political Rationalism* (ed. Thomas L. Pangle, Chicago 1989), in *The Times Literary Supplement*, No. 4522, pp. 1319–24 (December 1–7, 1989). Strauss is the most thoroughgoing modern exponent of the doctrines I describe, but there are many others.

12. *Hamlet*, III. ii. 19ff.

13. 'Burning', because light was a kind of fire. In the *Republic*, the eye borrows its fire from the Sun. F. M. Cornford, *The Republic of Plato*, Oxford University Press 1941, p. 219n., explains.

14. Martin Jay, 'In the Empire of the Gaze'; in David Couzens Hoy (ed.), *Foucault: A Critical Reader*, Blackwell 1986, pp. 175–204.

VI   Changing the World

1. On this, see Lyotard's *Le Différend*, cited above, II, n. 7; and Geoffrey Bennington, *Lyotard: Writing the Event*, Manchester University Press 1988.

2. Still the best piece of writing on this subject is Albert Schweitzer's magnificent late piece, 'The Conception of the Kingdom of God in the Transformation of Eschatology', first printed as an Appendix to E. N. Mozley's *The Theology of Albert Schweitzer*, 1950, and also to be found in Walter Kaufmann (ed.), *Religion from Tolstoy to Camus*, New York: Harper Torchbooks 1964.

3. Begun even before the English Revolution, with the Old Bedford River; but the full benefits came in after.

4. Adorno, in *The Dialectic of Enlightenment*, argues that the Enlightenment's impulse to rationalize, generalize and quantify everything led directly to the tyrannies of more recent times. Against it he sets the here-and-now, the particular and art.

5. On all this see Kate Soper, *Humanism and Anti-humanism*, Hutchinson 1986.

6. *Critique of Pure Reason*, B xiii (Kemp Smith translation).

7. Romans 11.33.

8. Hebrews 6.5.

9. Philippians 2.12.

10. Synergism is simply Greek for co-operation. The term was introduced by the moderate Reformer Philip Melanchthon. He put his claim very cautiously: the Spirit of God, converting the soul, permits the human will truly to co-operate with divine Grace. Up went the dry of 'Pelagianism!' – of course. My point is that the longstanding vehement desire to force the human will down into radical subordination is obviously driven by sexism. Which is blindingly obvious in the language used by Augustine, by Luther, by Calvin . . .

11. René Descartes, *Meditations on First Philosophy with selections from the Objections and Replies*, trans. John Cottingham, Cambridge University Press 1986, p. 17.

12. Ibid., p. 40.

13. Ibid., p. 32.

14. Bernard Williams, *Descartes: The Project of Pure Enquiry*, Penguin Books 1978, ch. 8, especially p. 246. Bernard Williams actually endorses the idea that scientific knowledge can be absolute knowledge. He accepts the Cartesian equations: scientific knowledge *equals* knowledge of the measurable, primary qualities of things *equals* knowledge of the characteristics of the material world as it really is *equals* absolute knowledge. But I ask, *why* this marvellous finalistic harmony between the way mathematical physicists' minds work and the way the objective world actually is? Is not the harmony obviously ideological, a necessary fiction assiduously propagated by physicists, but not something a philosopher should accept?

15. For Taylorism, see David Harvey, *The Condition of Postmodernity* (cited above, V, n. 6) pp. 125ff. The reference is to F. W. Taylor, *The Principles of Scientific Management*, New York 1911.

16. Noah Kennedy, *The Industrialization of Intelligence*, Unwin Hyman 1989.

17. The reference is to Ovid's *Metamorphoses*, and the curious fact that modern thought has scarcely yet taken up Ovid's suggestion that magical transformation is the central theme of myth.

18. E. W. Fuchs, *Richard Long*, Thames and Hudson 1986.

Index of Names

INDEX

INDEX